Discipling Through Theological
Education by Extension

Discipling Through Theological Education by Extension

*A fresh approach
to theological education
in the 1980s*

Edited by
Vergil Gerber

MOODY PRESS
CHICAGO

Library of Congress Cataloging in Publication Data
Main entry under title:

Discipling through theological education by extension.

  Includes bibliographical references.
  1. Seminary extension—Addresses, essays, lectures.
2. Theology—Study and teaching—Addresses, essays,
lectures. I. Gerber, Vergil.
BV4164.D57   207'.15   80-19327
ISBN 0-8024-2218-7

To
Raymond Buker, Sr.,

whose tireless efforts on behalf of theological education by extension around the world made his name synonomous with CAMEO (Committee to Assist Ministry Education Overseas), of which he served as coordinator until 1975

Contents

7

Foreword

I am delighted that Vergil Gerber has produced this particular book at this particular time. As it is read and digested by men and women involved in any way in the task of world evangelization; as it is translated into other languages and thereby influences leaders of Third World churches; and as the vital principles it articulates become part and parcel of practical programs for action on the grass-roots level—this book might well be used of God to initiate what I would like to think of as the Third Era in theological education by extension.

The *First Era* of theological education by extension (TEE) was a developmental phase. The original experiment conducted by Ross Kinsler, James Emery, and Ralph Winter in Guatemala spanned the years 1962-67. A successful model was needed, and that model was provided by the Presbyterian Seminary in Guatemala.

The *Second Era* of TEE began with a conference in Armenia, Colombia, in 1967. It was an era in which the movement spread worldwide. TEE first began to take hold through several of the Latin American republics, then became known on other continents largely through the efforts of Raymond Buker, Sr., to whom this volume is dedicated. As the coordinator of CAMEO (Committee to Assist Ministry Education Overseas), Buker organized key workshops and sent personnel all over the world to spread the TEE news.

And it caught. The idea of training those whom God had already called to the ministry and training them in their own communities rather than requiring them to travel long distances and live in a residential institution was a novelty to many, but it made sense. Denomination after denomination in country after country began taking the professors to the students rather than bringing the students to the professors. Although no accurate count can be taken, estimates of the number of leaders involved in training through TEE now run over twenty-five thousand, and some of them almost double that number. We are still in the Second Era.

However, the burden of this book, which I heartily endorse, is that a *Third Era* is urgently needed. The structure of TEE was developed and diffused throughout the world in the First Era and the Second Era. It is time now to concentrate on the content. What is TEE *for?* To introduce ministers to principles of biblical interpretation?—yes. To cause them to wrestle with theological concepts and be aware of the development of Christian dogma throughout history and on the contemporary scene?—yes. To help them organize their thoughts into more logical and symmetrical sermons?—yes. To give them skills for administering the sacraments, counseling those who have problems, performing marriages and funerals, and managing the affairs of a local church?—yes. But those are all areas of study in traditional ministerial training programs, and they frequently have been carried over into TEE with little or no change.

The Third Era of TEE questions whether that has been adequate. It raises basic concerns of purpose and curriculum. It is not satisfied with any program of ministerial training that prepares people for maintenance—simply maintaining the status quo of the existing congregations. It argues that TEE should be geared to facilitating the completion of Jesus' Great Commission to make disciples of all nations. This book, better than anything previously published, explains how that can and should be done.

Vergil Gerber, world traveler and evangelical statesman, has succeeded in pulling together contributions from many of the evangelical stars in the TEE galaxy. I am excited, for example, that George Patterson's work is getting wider exposure—it is long overdue. Fred Holland of the Wheaton Graduate School is probably the leading theoretician of TEE at the moment, and his contribution—the first time it has appeared in print—is outstanding. An earlier book that Ralph Covell and I did together is now out of print, and I am happy to see that two of his excellent chapters will live on. Clark Scanlon, Avery Willis, Jr., Terry Hulbert, and Lois McKinney have all contributed valuable insights that together constitute a publishing event in the evangelical world.

Tying it all together and putting all the material in perspective are the chapters by Vergil Gerber. If our TEE programs enroll thousands but do not motivate and prepare men and women of God for the task of making disciples of all peoples and multiplying Christian churches—so what? Vergil Gerber drives the point home with extraordinary skill. His chapters tie the knot between TEE and church growth.

I sincerely hope that the Third Era of TEE has indeed arrived. My message to you who are reading this book for one reason or another can be summed up in three words: read—pray—act!

C. PETER WAGNER
Fuller Theological Seminary
Pasadena, California

Acknowledgments

I am deeply grateful to the authors and publishers who so generously granted permission to use, edit, and adapt their materials in this book:

Dr. Ralph Covell's chapters were previously published in Ralph R. Covell and C. Peter Wagner, *An Extension Seminary Primer* (South Pasadena: William Carey Library, 1971).

Dr. A. Clark Scanlon's material has been culled and edited from various parts of his excellent book *Church Growth through Theological Education in Guatemala,* published in Guatemala in 1962 and now out of print.

Dr. Fred Holland's chapter is a condensation of several parts of his doctoral thesis, "Theological Education in Context and Change," D. Miss. dissertation, Fuller School of World Mission, 1978.

Dr. George Patterson's first chapter has been edited and adapted from his helpful little booklet *Obedience-Oriented Education* (Imprenta Misionera, P.O. Box 11586, Portland, Oregon 97211; 1976, rev. 1978). The second is a paper released by EMIS (Evangelical Missions Information Service) in 1974 as a special edition of *Latin America Pulse*.

Dr. Avery T. Willis, Jr., first published his fine treatise on contextualization in *Asian Perspective No. 8* (Republic of China [Taiwan]: Asia Theological Association, n.d.).

Dr. Terry Hulbert's material was first given at the Triennial Convention of the

Association of Evangelicals for Africa and Madagascar, which was held in the Ivory Coast in 1977, and later appeared in two subsequent issues of the *Evangelical Missions Quarterly,* July 1978, January 1979.

Dr. Lois McKinney's contribution, "Leadership: Key to Growth of the Church," was given as a major address at the Annual Convention of the Evangelical Foreign Missions Association in Orlando, Florida, in March 1979.

I am also very much indebted to my faithful and efficient wife, Dorothy, and to Georgia Douglass for the long and arduous hours they put into the typing and preparing of this book for publication.

Introduction

Theological education is never an end in itself. Its form and function are determined by its ultimate purpose. That purpose is succinctly stated in the answer to the first question in the Westminster Shorter Catechism:

Man's chief end *is to glorify God, and to enjoy him forever.*

Theology is the study of God. *Theological education* is the process by which a man learns to know God personally, to love Him with all his mind— and heart—and soul—and strength, and to glorify Him with his whole being.

But how do we glorify God? How do we know when we have fulfilled that chief end for our lives? Jesus said,

By this is My Father glorified,
that you bear much fruit,
and so prove to be My disciples . . .
You did not choose Me,
but I chose you, and appointed you,
that you should go and bear fruit,
and that your fruit should remain,
that whatever you ask of the Father
in My name, He may give to you
[John 15:8, 16].

The task is not completed until the discipled person has himself become a discipler of others.

Discipling disciplers is the ultimate goal of all theological education.

15

Theological Education in the 1980s:
Two Scenarios

Lois McKinney

SCENARIO 1: BOB AND JOAN

Seminary, U.S.A.
January 6, 1980

Dear Mom and Dad,

My second term here at seminary has just begun. I've signed up for fifteen credits again. That's the maximum load we're allowed to carry. If I could stand the thought of staying around here an extra year or two I'd cut down my course load to improve my grades. The competition is really keen, especially in Greek, where all the guys keep trying to outdo each other.

Greek isn't really all that hard if I could give more time to it. But I'm taking four other courses (Biblical Introduction, Church History, Hermeneutics, and Homiletics). Besides, I'm working thirty hours a week to try to keep up with my tuition, room and board, and car payments.

I had hoped to get on top of my bills over the Christmas break, but—wouldn't you know it—my car transmission went out. Good-bye, extra earnings.

I think I could handle my schoolwork and my job OK if that was all I was doing. But Joan and I are spending a lot of time together lately. She's really a great girl.

It bothers me that I'm not more involved in church life. I'm still working with high school kids at First Memorial, but I wonder if I should give it up. I'm never with them except on Sunday evenings. And there are plenty of others who could work with those kids if I dropped out.

What I would really like to do is to try my hand at starting a church in a new housing development near the seminary. That would be good preparation for the mission field. But I'm spread so thin already that I don't see how I can take on anything that would involve such a high degree of commitment. And I need more experience before I can expect to be ready to plant churches. My goal right now is to master Greek and theology and develop some preaching skills. I guess intensive involvement in ministry will have to wait until after I've completed my M.Div. and have been ordained.

21

My classes this term are disappointing. It's incredible that the higher you climb on the academic ladder, the worse the teaching is. I'm getting tired of boring lectures. Dr. Smith, the Hermeneutics professor, doesn't even touch on current issues. The father of one of the guys studied here twenty-three years ago, and he says Smith was saying the same things then.

I'm already behind on the readings and assignments. Most of them seem so irrelevant. Maybe they would make better sense if I were more involved in ministry.

I'm not sure that's the whole problem, though. It just dawned on me the other day that most of our profs aren't much more involved in churches than I am.

I'm sorry I couldn't get home for Christmas. I miss both of you, and I miss New England. Life is sure different here.

There's a Greek exam tomorrow, so I'll have to close. Write soon.

Love,

Bob and Joan

Mission Field
Latin America
January 6, 1989

Dear Mom and Dad,

It seems impossible that we've been back on the field for over a year. But here we are, ready to begin another semester at the seminary.

We've just tucked the children in bed. Joan is putting some finishing touches on the English course she'll be teaching. That's a course these Latin American students really appreciate.

I'll be teaching Introduction to Greek, Greek II, Greek Exegesis, Hermeneutics, and Ecclesiology. I've taught the Greek courses several times, so they won't take much preparation. And I found old syllabi from my seminary days that I'll be able to translate and use for the other two courses. I'm certainly glad I ran into these, because I'm taking over the seminary administration while Joe is on furlough. I won't have much time for class preparation.

We've had quite a few discipline problems in the dorm this year. Mario and Claudia handled the dorm for us before we lost them. Now Joan and I are back in our houseparent role again.

On the brighter side, I'm really pleased with our seminary's new curriculum. We based it on the best of what we found in seminary catalogs in the States. Our students seem pleased to know that they are getting exactly the same kind of training they would in North America.

I only wish we had more students. This year we have seven men and five women. God just doesn't seem to be calling many young people into the ministry these days. Most of them want to go to universities to prepare for other professions.

We're in our usual financial bind. It takes $50,000 a year to keep our school going. That doesn't include support for four missionary couples and two single missionaries. Right now all of us are undersupported, and the seminary special project fund is $30,000 in the red.

We got some disappointing news the other day. Do you remember us telling you about Jose? We had such high hopes for him when he studied here. I don't think I've ever had a better Greek student. Well, we just found out he's leaving the ministry to take a government job. I'm afraid his problem was pride. He just couldn't seem to identify with the people in his rural church. But he was *such* a good student.

Joan and I were hoping we could get involved in church planting this term. We really feel we're out of touch with what's happening around us. But, as Joan said when we were talking about this a few weeks ago, "*Somebody* has to keep the seminary going!" So it looks as if that's what we'll be doing, at least for the rest of this term.

Please keep praying. We both get discouraged at times.

Love always,

Bob and Joan

Scenario 2: Dan and Ruth

Seminary, U.S.A.
January 6, 1980

Dear Mom and Dad,

So much has happened since Ruth and I have been here at seminary that I hardly know where to begin. We've grown so much and in so many ways. I've forgotten what I've already told you about our program. Let me try to explain how it functions.

We began with a series of orientation seminars. Each of us took a long look at himself in the light of what God is doing in his life. We talked about many things: where we are right now; where we would like to be ten years from now; where we need to grow. Then we developed a growth contract, with the help and encouragement of a guidance committee.

Ruth and I had talked about our goals several times with our group at First Church. You may remember how much we valued the reassurance of God's call that came from them. So it wasn't hard for us to look ahead. We saw ourselves involved in church leadership development in a Latin American country.

We decided that if we want to be able to develop leaders for Latin American churches, we need to become effective church leaders ourselves. We'll need a good foundation in Bible, theology, church history, and so on. But, as Prof. Evans explained, it makes better sense to learn in the context of ministry. So we are working with a team that is trying to plant and help develop a church. Our team members get together at least once a week to reflect on what is happening in our lives and in our ministries. We try to relate our reading and study to what we are experiencing. Our curiosity about the ordinances and polities of our denomination sent us back through church history and through several works on ecclesiology. Ruth and I have been trying to help a young divorcee who has been coming to one of the Bible study groups. It has really made us struggle with cultural and ethical issues. It's also sharpened our counseling skills and Bible knowledge.

I forgot to mention that two of our profs are a part of our church-planting team. I've learned more by watching them in action than I would ever learn from them in a classroom.

We seldom have lectures. We get most of our information through our own study and research, or through cassettes and videotapes. We tell each other what we've learned when our team gets together.

So here we are, studying and growing together while we work together to build up the church. Sometimes I almost forget this is a seminary. We hear a lot about "growth goals" and "competencies" and very little about grades or credits.

In case you haven't guessed it by now, this program has both of us really excited.

More later,

Dan and Ruth

Mission Field
Latin America
January 6, 1989

Dear Mom and Dad,

Ruth and I have just come back from our weekly meeting with the seminary students. That is always an exciting time of hearing what is happening in their ministries.

You'll remember that those students are all mature, proved leaders of their churches. They are enrolled in seminary because their churches have recognized their spiritual gifts. The extension program makes it possible for them to live and work in their own communities while they are studying.

The program revolves around a weekly encounter. Everyone is full of things he wants to tell about. Last night Sergio and Maria told us that the congregation they are working with has outgrown the home they have been meeting in. They are helping some of the key leaders begin another group.

Joaquim reported that believers in the church he is helping to pastor have been busy presenting the gospel to their relatives and neighbors. There have been twenty decisions for Christ this month. Most of the new converts are related. Everyone seems to be someone's cousin or aunt or brother—or at least a compadre! The believers worship and study together, and they encourage each other to reach out in ministries of evangelism and compassion. Simplicity of structures is a must when a nation's economy has collapsed.

The shattered economy has made churches here take their caring ministries seriously. Evangelicals have banded together in a relief program to provide food, clothing, and jobs for immigrants who are flooding into the city from the rural areas. Working with the program has made the students ask themselves questions about poverty and life-style and suffering. I'm delighted with the solid biblical perspective they bring to the discussions. They are doing a great job of developing a biblically-based, culturally-contextualized theology.

Ruth and the children are well. In our family prayer-time last night, Dan, Jr. thanked the Lord for giving him such a happy Mommy and Daddy. We *are* happy. There has never been another time in our lives when we have experienced more personal fulfillment in our ministry. Thank you for praying.

Love always,

Dan and Ruth

* * * * *

Theological educators in the 1980s are likely to teach as they have been taught.

Discipling

1

Discipling Through Theological Education by Extension

Vergil Gerber

Ask the average Christian in the pew or the average missionary on the field today what is meant by *evangelism* and you may get as many answers as you have people. Replies will run the gamut from "giving a stranger a gospel tract" to "political involvement in the struggle for human rights."

Although the King James Version of the evangelistic mandate to the church in Matthew 28:19-20 says, "Go . . ., and teach all nations," the double imperative[1] and the use of the word *teach* for two very different Greek verbs[2] somewhat obscure the exact meaning of this Great Commission. But the original Greek text leaves no room for doubt as to what is meant. It clearly defines the task of evangelism as *making disciples*. "Going," says a literal rendering, "you are to make disciples among all nations, baptizing and teaching them." Nothing short of *disciples* fulfills the evangelistic objective.

VERGIL GERBER (M.Div., Northern Baptist Theological Seminary; D.D., Conservative Baptist Theological Seminary) is executive director of Evangelical Missions Information Service, headquartered in Wheaton, Illinois. Serving under the Conservative Baptist Foreign Mission Society and the Conservative Baptist Home Mission Society since 1948, Dr. Gerber has conducted evangelism/church growth workshops in fifty countries.

DISCIPLE!

In the little, heart-shaped country of Burundi nestled deep in the Central African hills, some fifty national pastors grappled with the profound implications of that central imperative of the Great Commission. It was their first exposure to a workshop in evangelism and church growth, and they were bristling with questions.

Who makes disciples? God alone! In fact, no one *makes* disciples. You cannot force people to become disciples. And you cannot carve them from a tree in the forests. Our Bible institutes and theological seminaries do not produce them. Disciples are created by God. Yet (the pastors continued wrestling with the concept), clearly the task has been committed to *us*. We, His church, are commanded to make disciples.

"But we don't even have a word in the Kirundi language for the verb *disciple*," they argued. "You just can't say it in our native tongue." As they pondered the meaning of the divine imperative, suddenly one pastor stood to his feet, his black face beaming. "I know what this means, but it will take three Kirundi words to express it instead of one: *change people disciples.*"

EVANGELISM IS CHANGING PEOPLE INTO DISCIPLES!
ACTS 14

In the fourteenth chapter of the Acts of the Apostles we have the report of that outstanding New Testament evangelistic team, Paul and Barnabas, whom

God used so mightily throughout Asia Minor. Great things were happening in city after city—the "people centers" of that day.

Verse 1. First, they came to Iconium. The word used to describe the action of the evangelistic team here is *laleo*. They *spoke* in the synagogue. What were they doing? Evangelizing. And their evangelistic effectiveness was measured by tangible results—by people who were *changed into disciples*. "A great multitude of people believed." The New International Version puts it this way: "They spoke so effectively that a great number of Jews and Gentiles believed." Their witness was public and oral. And their results were tangible disciples.

Verses 6-7. Next the evangelistic team traveled to Lystra, a city of Lycaonia. And there also they "continued to preach the gospel." The Greek word here, however, is not *laleo* (speak) or *kerusso* (preach or proclaim), but *evaggelizomai*—evangelize! They evangelized the city.

Verse 15. Here again we find "preach the gospel," and the verb is *evaggelizomenoi*—evangelizing. Then notice an exciting new dimension. I like to call it "expectant evangelism." They did not just preach the gospel. They *expected* a response. They *expected* men to turn from their idols ("these vain things") to the living God. They *expected* to see people changed into disciples.

Verses 20-21. Their next stop was Derbe. The *New American Standard Bible* reads: "And after they had preached the gospel . . . and had made many disciples." A literal translation of the original Greek would be, "when they had evangelized [*evaggelizomenoi*] . . . having made many disciples [*matheteusantes*—passive participle] they returned to Lystra and Iconium."

Verse 22. Their goal was to confirm and establish the converts they had made—relating them to other disciples, bringing them together, solidifying them into new Christian communities (nuclei of disciples, probably small house-congregations like the one in the house of Cornelius, mentioned in Acts 10). Paul and Barnabas made sure that the converts were *individually* firmly established and grounded. And they exhorted and challenged them to continue in their newfound faith before going on.

Verse 23. Furthermore, they made sure that *collectively* the converts would continue on as a group of believers. To achieve that they helped them select and appoint leadership in each church. According to Thayer, the Greek word *cheirotonesantes* indicates that the appointment of presbyters (elders) was by vote by the raising or stretching of hands.

Verses 24-25. Once that was accomplished and the new thriving groups of disciples were in competent hands, Paul and Barnabas commended them to the Lord and moved on to other "people centers," where they followed the same pattern of evangelism. *Paul and Barnabas did not consider their evangelistic task complete until a church was firmly planted and had taken root in each place.*

Verses 26-27. Now we see them returning to Antioch. Here they gathered together the church, the group of disciples who had thrust them out on their evangelistic mission in the first place, and they told them what God had been doing.

Verse 28. *Disciples* and *church* are interchangeable terms. In verse 27 Luke speaks of the disciples as "the church." Here in the very next verse he refers to them as "the disciples."

It is interesting to note that the term *Christian* (that is, one who belongs to or is a follower of Christ) was used for the first time in relation to the disciples at Antioch (Acts 11:26). Nowhere in the historical record does the term appear prior to the establishing of the church in Antioch, not even in relation to the first church in Jerusalem. In fact, Young's concordance lists only three times where the term *Christian* appears at all in the entire New Testament.[3] And in each of these three occasions, the term is used synonymously with *disciple.*

From our study thus far, three things become indelibly evident from the Scriptures:

1. *Evangelism and discipling in the New Testament are inseparably linked together.* Every place Paul and Barnabas went, their evangelistic effectiveness was measured not by *decisions,* but by *disciples*—not by the preaching of the *message,* but by the producing of *men* who wholly followed the Lord.

2. *Evangelism and discipling in the New Testament focus on the church.* Christ loved the church and gave Himself for it (Eph. 5:25). His evangelistic purposes are centered in the church (Matt. 16:18—"I will build My church"). His primary concern is for His church (John 17). The evangelistic mandate (Matt. 28:19-20) is given *to* the church and is to be carried out *by* the church (John 17:20). He prays for those who will believe through *their* word. The church is not only the *object* but also the

agent of New Testament evangelism. Disciples, who make up the church, are His method. On the Day of Pentecost, as a result of the preaching of the gospel, the Lord added 3,000 to the little band of 120 disciples who made up the charter members of the first church in Jerusalem (Acts 2:41). And through the believers' witness the Lord continued to add new disciples ("those who were being saved") to the church daily (Acts 2:47). Note that it was *to the church* that they were added.

3. *Evangelism and discipling in the New Testament are not complete until:*
   a) Converts are incorporated into churches
   b) Churches have been firmly planted and have taken root in every part of the world.

On the Day of Pentecost, the Holy Spirit brought the church into being and launched her on her evangelistic course. Those who were converted by the preaching of the gospel were immediately baptized and incorporated into the Jerusalem *koinonia.* From that day on, dynamic, living cells—nuclei of disciples—began to multiply into hundreds of congregations in Asia, Europe, Africa, and around the world. The Acts of the Apostles records the astounding story of evangelistic success as men like Paul and Barnabas saw their God-given evangelistic task in that two-fold dimension.

Now let us take a closer look at the use of the word *disciple* in the New Testament.

WHAT DO WE MEAN BY *DISCIPLE?*

The English word *disciple* occurs 264 times in the King James Version of the New Testament. Of those occurrences, 234 appear in the four gospels and 30 are found in the Acts of the Apostles. In every instance the word is used in the form of a noun.[4]

Thayer's Greek lexicon, however, lists five occurrences of the Greek verb *matheteuo* (to disciple or to make a disciple).[5] Two of these are used as an intransitive verb in connection with Joesph of Arimathea: "who himself had also become a disciple of Jesus" (Matt. 27:57) and "being a disciple of Jesus" (John 19:38). A third occurrence refers to "every scribe who has become a disciple of the kingdom of heaven" (Matt. 13:52). As we have already seen, the context of the fourth instance, Acts 14:21, implies that the evangelistic process is a means to an end, the making of disciples: "And after they had preached the gospel [evangelized] . . . and had made many disciples, they returned to Lystra and to Iconium and to Antioch."

The only instance in which *matheteuo* is used in the imperative tense, however, is in Matthew's version of the Great Commission (Matt. 28:19). Here Jesus clearly spells out the marching orders of the church: disciple all nations! It is not *didasko,* as in verse 20, which simply means "to impart instruction," that is, "to teach"; rather, it is *matheteuo,* which implies a definite commitment on the part of the one discipled, both to his master and to the precepts his master lays down. It implies a resultant change of one's way of living. In verse 20 "teaching" becomes the means to an end. In verse 19, the imperative "make disciples" becomes an end in itself.

Turning to the noun form, the simplest meaning of the Greek word *mathetes* is "a learner." It suggests a pupil-teacher relationship. However, as you trace the usage of the word through the gospels and the Acts of the Apostles, you will discover that the pupil-teacher relationship soon becomes a servant-master relationship implying a commitment of obedience both to the master-teacher himself and to the precepts and instruction that he has imparted. *The International Standard Bible Encyclopædia* says:

> In all cases it implies that the person not only accepts the views of the teacher, but that he is also in practice an adherent. The word has several applications. In the widest sense it refers to those who accept the teachings of anyone, not only in belief but in life. Thus the disciples of John the Baptist (Mt **9** 14; Lk **7** 18; Jn **3** 25); also of the Pharisees (Mt **22** 16; Mk **2** 18; Lk **5** 33); of Moses (Jn **9** 28). But its most common use is to designate the adherents of Jesus. . . . It is the only name for Christ's followers in the Gospels. . . . In the Acts, after the death and ascension of Jesus, disciples are those who confess Him as the Messiah, Christians (Acts **6** 1.2.7; **9** 36 [fem., *mathêtria*]; **11** 26 . . .). Even half-instructed believers who had been baptized only with the baptism of John are disciples (Acts **19** 1-4).[6]

To be *discipled* therefore implies both a commitment and a process. Indeed, the commitment of faith forms the bridge between evangelism and discipling.

Commitment of Faith

EVANGELISM → DISCIPLING

It is both an initial act and a continuing experience. As you trace the use of the word *mathetes* through the gospels and the Acts, you will discover at least six areas to which the disciple of Jesus Christ is committed:

1. HE IS COMMITTED TO CHRIST

The word *didaskalos* (teacher) is almost exclusively translated "master" throughout the gospels and the Acts of the Apostles, and it beautifully pictures that commitment to Christ. Christ is not merely our teacher. He is our master, our Lord, to whom we have committed our lives. It is that commit-

That is also graphically illustrated in the figure of the Body, in which each member—each disciple—is intimately related to Christ, the head. *He* controls our actions. *He* directs our lives. *He* instructs each member. *He* causes each member to function in his respective area or responsibility. Every true disciple places himself in subjection to his master.

Luke 14:26-27, 33: "If anyone comes to Me, and does not hate his own father and mother and wife and children and brothers and sisters, yes, and even his own life, he cannot be My disciple. Whoever does not carry his own cross and come after Me cannot be My disciple. . . . So therefore, no one of you can be My disciple who does not give up all his own possessions."

Matthew 27:57: "And when it was evening, there came a rich man from Arimathea, named Joseph, who himself had also become a disciple of Jesus." *The International Standard Bible Encyclopædia* makes the literal rendition "was discipled to Jesus."[7] The use of the passive tense with the dative of the person whose disciple one is made implies that Joseph of Arimathea was discipled *to* or *unto* Jesus, not *by* Him. One might well read the King James translation in that sense of commitment when it simply says, "Joseph, who also himself was Jesus' disciple."

Although it is true that John's version in 19:38 states that Joseph's commitment was "a disciple of Jesus, but a secret [or hidden] one, for fear of the Jews," one must recognize that his commitment was both an act and a process involving a transitional, developing period. *The International Standard Bible Encyclopædia* describes Joseph as

> A "rich man" (Mt **27** 57), "a councillor of honorable estate," or member of the Sanhedrin (Mk **15** 43; Lk **23** 50), "a good and righteous man. . . . who was looking for the kingdom of God" (Lk **23** 50; Mk **15** 43), and "himself was Jesus' disciple" (Mt **27** 57; Jn **19** 38). Although he kept his discipleship secret [for the time being] "for fear of the Jews" (Jn **19** 38), he was yet faithful to his allegiance in that he absented himself from the meeting which found Jesus guilty of death (cf Lk **23** 51; Mk **14** 64). But the condemnation of his Lord awakened the courage and revealed the true faith of J. [I.e., his commitment of faith.] On the evening after the crucifixion he went "boldly" to Pilate and begged the body of Jesus.[8]

The Expositor's Greek New Testament further elaborates:

> This required some courage on Joseph's part. . . . "These Jewish aristocrats first confess Him in the hour of His deepest degradation." Plummer. Nicodemus is identified [with Him] as . . ., "he who came to Jesus by night at the first"; [John] iii. i. in contrast to the boldness of his coming now.[9]

But the examples of both Joseph and Nicodemus in no way alter the standard and profile of what New Testament discipleship should involve. And the evidence is clear that in the end there was a total commitment to Jesus as master of their lives.

2. HE IS COMMITTED TO THE CHURCH

Disciples are inherently committed *to* the church. They intrinsically become a part *of* the church. As members of the body, they are intimately related to other members within the body and are therefore committed to each other. There is no such thing as discipleship isolated from the body. A human body cannot be severed from its head, and therefore commitment to Christ as head is commitment also to His body, the church.

Out of the evangelism and church-growth workshops we have now conducted in nearly fifty nations of the world, a new concept has emerged: *body evangelism.* The term distinguishes the new approach from almost all other kinds of evangelism in that it is *goal*-oriented rather than *method*-oriented.

Most contemporary terms like *saturation evangelism, explosion evangelism, mobilization evangelism, coffeehouse evangelism, personal evangelism* and *crusade evangelism,* describe methods.

Body evangelism focuses on the goal of making disciples who are committed not only to Christ but also to the body of Christ. In keeping with Christ's command, it insists on building into all evangelistic efforts the biblical pattern of *follow-through*: baptizing and adding those who receive Christ to the local body of disciples and making them responsible, reproducing church members who in turn make responsible, reproducing churches.

Responsible, reproducing Christians

Responsible, reproducing churches

Just as a literal translation of Matthew 13:52 speaks of every scribe "instructed [or discipled—*matheteutheis*] into the kingdom of heaven" so we may speak of "being discipled *into* the church."

Acts 2:41 tells us that those who gladly accepted the message were baptized in public commitment of their identification *with* the local body of believers in Jerusalem and that they were incorporated *into* their fellowship. They were added *to* the church (v. 41) and continued steadfastly *in* the apostles' doctrine (*didache*—teaching) and fellowship *(koinonia),* and in the breaking of bread and in prayers (v. 42). In verse 47 we see them "praising God [together], and having favor with all the people [members of the body]. And the Lord was adding to their number day by day those who were being saved."

Evangelism that disciples men into the local church is the New Testament norm. And in Acts 14:27-28 and 11:26, as we have already seen, *disciples* is used interchangeably with *the church* and with *Christians.* In its biblical-

41

historical development, there is no such thing as New Testament Christianity apart from the church.

3. HE IS COMMITTED TO THE WORD

Both *evangelism* and its more inclusive synonym *discipleship* are dependent upon the authoritative word of the Master and of His holy apostles. [10] The instructions and precepts of that word are embodied in Holy Scripture, which in the original autographs is inerrant and therefore wholly trustworthy as an infallible guide. Disciples are committed to that Word. The continuous application of the Word to the life of the one discipled is the test of discipleship.

John 8:31—"If you abide in My word, then you are truly disciples of Mine."

Acts 2:41-42—Those who gladly received the Word and were baptized and added to the church also continued receiving instruction (*didache*—teaching) in the church. Their commitment to the Word was both an initial and a continuing experience. And their theological education was an essential part of the church's ministry.

4. HE IS COMMITTED TO OTHER MEMBERS IN THE BODY

There is in the church a collective, horizontal relationship that makes disciples responsible *to* and *for* each other. And that commitment is evident to everyone, both within and without the church.

John 13:35—"By this all men will know that you are My disciples, if you have love for one another." The very word *koinonia* implies much more than a closely-knit fellowship of kindred minds. The root meaning of the word is "to have in common." The word means *caring* to the point of *sharing*. When one member of the body suffers, all suffer. When one member rejoices, all members rejoice. (1 Cor. 12:25-26).

Acts 2:44-45—"And all those who had believed [disciples] were together, and had all things in common [*koina*]; and they began selling their property and possessions, and were sharing them with all, as anyone might have need."

5. HE IS COMMITTED TO REPRODUCE

The commitment to reproduce is graphically illustrated for us in the analogy

42

of the vine and the branches given in John 15. The Master is the vine. The disciples are the branches. The relationship is described in terms of *purpose* and *function*. It is set forth in the context of reproduction.

In verse 5 the Master reveals that the branches share the life of the vine and He in turn shares their life. That is what is meant by abiding in Him. And the result is fruit. His life flows through them. It continuously sends out new, tender shoots on the branches. They in turn produce new fruit. That is the purpose for which they have been related to the vine.

In verse 8 there is a *purpose* clause introduced by a little purpose conjunction *hena*. Here is the purpose: "that you bear much fruit." The *Good News Bible* translates the verse this way: "My Father's glory is shown by your bearing much fruit; and in this way you become my disciples."

6. HE IS COMMITTED TO THE WORSHIP AND MINISTRY OF THE CHURCH

The record of the early church makes it clear that the early disciples were committed not only to Christ and to each other but also to the worship and ministry of the church.

Acts 2:41-47—The disciples continued steadfastly meeting regularly ("day by day"—v. 46) in the Temple, breaking bread from house to house, receiving instruction, praying, and praising God together.

Acts 20:7 says that "on the first day of the week"—what had come to be set apart as belonging to the Master—the disciples were "gathered together to break bread," and Paul preached to them. The Greek word used here is not *kerusso,* the usual word for preach, or *evaggelizomai* ("evangelize," usually translated "preach the gospel") but *dia-legomai*—that is, "lectured" or "talked to." By that time the custom of assembling together for a discourse from the Word was firmly established "on the first day of the week." That was preceded by the "breaking of the bread," which later became known as the Lord's Supper.

The writer to the Hebrews reminded his audience of their commitment to those special times set aside for worship, fellowship, and instruction by the early disciples when he cautioned them, "Not forsaking our own assembling together" (Heb. 10:25).

In addition to worship, the early disciples were also committed to the *ministry* of the church. In addressing the church in Ephesus, Paul reminded the disciples both of their unity and of their responsibility in the church.

Ephesians 4:11-12—Who carries out the work of the ministry? Paul pointed out that it is not the primary responsibility of those gifted and chosen to lead the church, but of *every* disciple. It is the work of the saints. And every disciple must share his responsibility in the "work of the ministry" (KJV).

Evangelism is the central task of the church, the heart and core of the work of the ministry. It is not the task of a few paid professionals; rather, it is the responsibility of the *whole* church—of *every* disciple.

ELEMENTS ESSENTIAL TO DISCIPLESHIP IN THE FULFILLMENT OF THE EVANGELISTIC MANDATE

When does a disciple become a disciple? Is it when he makes a decision in response to an evangelistic invitation? Or is it when he attains a certain level of maturity? At what point on the continuum from the initial decision to the perfected disciple does one pass the test of biblical discipleship?

CONTINUUM OF DISCIPLESHIP

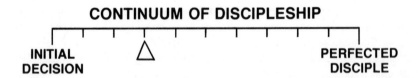

INITIAL
DECISION

PERFECTED
DISCIPLE

Even a superficial reading of the gospels and the Acts at that point will reveal a wide disparity in the use of the word from the simplest definition of a "learner" or "follower" to the highest ideal of the perfected saint. There is a point on the continuum, however, where certain basic elements are essential to the fulfillment of the evangelistic mandate. Although a disciple as a "learner" never ceases to be "instructed," at least in this life, and we are enjoined by the writer to the Hebrews to "press on to maturity" (Heb. 6:1), there are certain steps of commitment and responsibility that are indispensable to the life of *every* disciple if he is to fulfill the requirements inherent in the Great Commission. And the New Testament gives us a visual model to follow. It is set in the context of the historical development of the evangelistic purpose of God for this age—which centers in the church.

Let me suggest four key words to help us visualize that historic development:

1. *Purpose*. Matthew 16:18: "I will build My church." The evangelistic goal is clearly stated. It is *His* church made up of *His* disciples.

2. *Plan*. Matthew 28:19: *"Make disciples."* The master blueprint concentrates on a single imperative for achieving that purpose. The verb forms used in those verses clearly distinguish between the means and the end to be achieved. Disciples are the end goal. The additional sheets in the blueprint (Mark 16:15; Luke 24:47-48; John 20:21; Acts 1:8) simply elaborate on the means by which the goal is to be attained.

3. *Profile*. Acts 2:41-47 gives us a model to go by and leaves no doubt as to what is meant by "building His church" and "making disciples" in the evangelistic context. The local visible body of believers in Jerusalem provides a clear profile of the elements vitally essential to the fulfillment of the disciple-making process projected in the master blueprint. Of course, "discipling" includes a great deal more, but the visual profile given here in the Jerusalem model points up the minimum basic requirements for fulfilling the plan of the master architect in the building of His church. What are they?

a. Conversion. Verse 41: "Those who had received his word." The initial decision to follow Christ is the door of entrance to discipleship. It is the beginning step rather than the end to be achieved in the evangelistic process.

b. Identification. Verse 41: They "were baptized." Public identification with the Master in His death, burial, and resurrection is the second indispensable requisite.

c. Incorporation. Verse 41: They "were added that day" to the church. Their identification was not simply with the Master but also with the church. They were incorporated into the newly formed body of disciples in Jerusalem.

d. Instruction. Verse 42: They were instructed in and by the church. The early church *gathered* for the purpose of instruction, that they might in turn be *scattered* to fulfill their evangelistic mandate.

e. Involvement. Verses 42-46: They were actively involved in the ministry of the church. They were intimately related to each other in worship and service.

f. Propagation. Verse 47: They reached out into the community. Their discipling was not inbred or stagnant. It was not self-centered; it was others-centered. *Koinonia* for them meant caring for others in need and telling others about their faith, as the root meaning of the word conveys. The church was not a closed fellowship of the elite or of the elect.

g. Reproduction. Verse 47: They gained the favor of those outside the church, and "the Lord was adding to their number day by day those who were being saved."

4. *Pattern.* Acts 6 through the rest of the historic record. Out of the Jerusalem model developed a standard pattern of evangelism and disciple-making. From that point onward, thriving new disciple cells began to emerge and in turn to spread the *evangelion* to other parts of the then-known world like tiny embers that are fanned into a mighty conflagration. The Jerusalem church multiplied into hundreds of visible congregations throughout Asia, Europe, Africa, and the rest of the world.

Disciples Are at the Heart of His Church

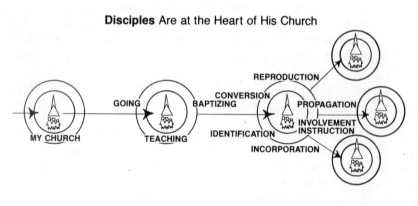

PURPOSE	PLAN	PROFILE	PATTERN
aiming at the MARK	The evangelizing MANDATE	The Jerusalem MODEL	N.T. MULTIPLICATION
Matt. 16:18	Matt. 28:19-20	Acts 2:41-47	Acts 6

The New Testament records make it perfectly obvious that to *disciple* in the

46

context of the evangelistic mandate is to make responsible, reproducing *Christians* who in turn make responsible, reproducing *congregations*.

Discussion Questions

1. How are the terms *evangelism* and *discipling* related? Discuss their similarities and their differences. In what way are they related to the church?
2. When does a disciple become a disciple? What elements of discipleship are indispensable in fulfilling the Great Commission? What does it mean to disciple a nation?
3. Discuss the practical implication of *biblical discipleship* on the philosophy, purpose, and program of theological education.

1. Actually there is only one imperative in Matthew's version of the Great Commission: *matheteusate*, which is translated in the King James Version as "teach" and which means "disciple." All the other words are auxiliary to that primary task. They are given to us in the form of dependent participles that modify the subject of the main verb and assist in the completion of the principal action.
2. *Matheteuo* (disciple) is used in verse 19, while *didasko* (instruct) is used in verse 20.
3. Once in Acts 11:26, in reference to the disciples (the church) at Antioch; once in Acts 26:28, when King Agrippa said to Paul, "In a short time you will persuade me to become a Christian [or disciple]"; and once in 1 Peter 4:16, where Peter speaks of a follower of Christ's suffering (being persecuted) because he is a Christian.
4. Robert Young, *Analytical Concordance to the Bible*, 20th ed. (New York: Funk & Wagnalls, n.d.).
5. Joseph Henry Thayer, *A Greek-English Lexicon of the New Testament* (New York: American Book Co., 1889).
6. James Orr, ed., *The International Standard Bible Encyclopaedia* (Grand Rapids: Eerdmans, 1939), 2:851.
7. Ibid., 2:851.
8. Ibid., 3:1741.
9. Marcus Dods, "John's Gospel," in W. Robertson Nicoll, ed., *The Expositor's Greek New Testament* (Grand Rapids: Eerdmans, n.d.), 1:860-61.
10. A *synonym,* according to *Webster's New Collegiate Dictionary,* is "one of two or

more words or expressions of the same language that have the same or nearly the same meaning in some or all senses.'' Although *evangelism* and *discipleship* in this frame of reference are synonymous, the terms have different connotations. *Evangelism* is the process by which men and women enter into a new relationship as disciples in the body of Christ. *Making disciples* is a broader term that embodies the evangelistic task in that initial commitment but also includes continuing experience related to the process of sanctification.

Just as the perfect tense of the Greek word *sesosmenoi* in Ephesians 2:5 and 8 indicates both that we *have been saved* at a point of time in the past by an initial commitment of faith and that we *continue to be saved* in the present as an ongoing, personal, day-by-day experience, so we can speak of disciples as *having been made* (Matt. 27:57) at a point of time, as by faith they enter into the initial commitment of discipleship, and at the same time as *being made* as they day-by-day ''grow in the grace and knowledge of our Lord'' (2 Pet. 3:18), being ''conformed to the image of His Son'' (Rom. 8:29) and our Master.

2

Discipling by Families:
A New Testament Pattern

Terry C. Hulbert

The family is a key factor in evangelism and church growth—a potential often overlooked or misunderstood. Winning entire households to Jesus Christ is not only a basic strategy in the growth of the church, but also one firmly rooted in Holy Scripture. Discipling by families is a New Testament pattern.

Household discipling involves two ideas:

1. The Christian home is the *means* of discipling the extended family and the community.
2. The non-Christian home is the *target* for discipling by families.

TERRY C. HULBERT (Th.D., Dallas Theological Seminary) is dean of Columbia Graduate School of Bible and Missions, Columbia, South Carolina. Dr. Hulbert has served as a missionary with the Africa Evangelical Fellowship. Recent overseas ministries have included church growth workshops with pastors in several African nations.

The Meaning of Household Discipling

Negatively, *household discipling* does not mean that children become Christians when their parents believe (although as Paul told the Corinthians, having parents who believe does give the children a spiritual advantage over children in a pagan home—1 Cor. 7:14). There is nothing automatic about salvation. We are not born into it because we are born into a Christian family.

Positively, *household discipling* is the basic decision by parents together, or by a father, to believe on the Lord Jesus Christ as Savior followed by consultation with other members of the family so that they, as individuals, likewise decide to come to Christ, resulting in a Christian family and household.[1]

As Dr. George Peters points out, household discipling has three basic features:

1. The family acts in deliberation and unity on the basic issue as explained from the Bible.
2. The decision is made under the direction and guidance of the parents, or of the father.
3. The members of the family old enough to do so make the decision consciously, voluntarily, and without pressure—and with the support of the family.[2]

The Relevance of Household Discipling

In a recent church-growth workshop in Sierra Leone, pastors discussed the importance of working through the family unit in evangelism. They said that it was not only courteous to go first to the head of a household, or tribal group, or village, but often very productive. They gave examples of evangelists who asked the person in authority for permission to show him what they proposed to teach. That procedure usually resulted in permission to make a presentation to the elders and people, who were thus exposed to the basics of the gospel in the process of determining if the message should be taught.

When the village leader gives permission to preach, people feel freer to receive the message than if their leader has been bypassed. Even when the ruler is resistant to the gospel, if he is approached with respect he will often give permission to teach it. What is true of a village situation applies also to penetrating a household. A respectful approach to the head is appropriate and potentially very productive.

BIBLICAL EXAMPLES OF HOUSEHOLD DISCIPLING

1. IN THE GOSPELS

Jesus and the apostles often presented the gospel to a whole family or household together. The Scripture records that, as individuals, many or all of a household would turn to the Lord Jesus at almost the same time.

For instance, at the beginning of Jesus' ministry in Galilee, He healed the son of a Roman army officer (John 4:46-54). The father was actually in Cana, where he had come to find Jesus, and the son was sick at Capernaum, some twenty miles distant. The servants later told him that the son had been healed at the exact moment Jesus had pronounced him cured. As a result, "he himself believed, and his whole household" (John 4:53).[3] A Roman father and his family and workers were saved together, as each believed on Christ at about the same time.

Even more striking was the transformation in the household of a despised Jewish tax collector in the city of Jericho (Luke 19:1-10). In His method of evangelism, Jesus went beyond where we usually go today. *Zaccheus* probably believed while he was in a tree in downtown Jericho. He had sought Jesus; he apparently was willing to expose his heart to Him; and Jesus responded. Jesus did not need to go to Zaccheus's house to save him! But at that time of great pressure, when crowds were following Him to that last Passover in Jerusalem, Jesus insisted on going to Zaccheus's house.

We can imagine the family's shock as the prophet from Galilee walked in with the tax-collector father to whom no respectable Jew would speak. Zaccheus had "received Him gladly" (Luke 19:6) and, as a result, his whole family was to be introduced to the Savior. And they received Him, too, so that Jesus could say, "Today salvation has come to this house" (Luke 19:9).

That that included at least the family and probably the servants is indicated by Jesus' use of "house," for if only Zaccheus were meant, he alone would have been mentioned. The context also indicates that *oikos,* the Greek word used here, carries the sense of "household."[4] The next verse (Luke 19:10) notes that "the Son of Man has come to seek and to save that which was lost." Jesus had sought them as a family—in their house and through the head of the household! Because the Lord had gone into a home to evangelize, a man

51

who began the day as a troubled tax collector ended it as the head of a family of God's children.

2. IN THE BOOK OF ACTS AND IN THE EPISTLES

In the early church the household continued to be the focus of evangelism. For instance, Acts 2:46 says that was true of Jewish believers in Jerusalem. As a sequel to Pentecost they broke their bread by households. They shared the common food and experiences of the day, and they hallowed their fellowship by partaking of the tokens Jesus had given them for remembrance of Himself.

They did it not just in homes but by households—that is, by families.[5] That family units are in view is attested by F. F. Bruce's translation, "by households."[6] If many had been evangelized as families (Zaccheus, Stephanas, et al.) it would be natural to fellowship and worship by families—that is, there would be household churches.

In Acts 20:20 Luke records a similar situation among Gentile believers in Ephesus. Whole families had come to know the Lord together and were being taught together; Paul taught them publicly and by households.[7] Here again is the concept of household churches.

Cornelius lived at Caesarea, the Roman capital of the Middle East. He was a Roman army officer who had admired Jewish religious values and had been seeking the Jews' God. But he was a Gentile, a member of a people whom Jews called "dogs" and who, as a group, had not yet been touched by the news of redemption in the cross and power in the resurrection.

Cornelius not only waited himself for Peter to come, as he had been instructed, but also called together his family and friends to hear him (Acts 10:24, 33, 44-48). In a few short statements Peter reviewed the history of Israel, the meaning of the life and death of Christ, and the way to receive forgiveness of sins. As a result, Cornelius, his family, and his friends believed and were baptized and discipled. Note that the record mentions only Cornelius as seeking spiritual answers (Acts 10:1-2). His need could have been met in a private interview with Peter. But God so guided that a whole household heard the Word with him and, following his example, also came to know the Savior personally. This is an example of collective discipling.

Lydia lived in Philippi of Macedonia, in northeastern Greece, where she had established a fabric business (Acts 16:14-15). Perhaps she was a widow.

At least we are told that she had a house large enough to accommodate Paul, Silas, Luke, and Timothy. God had opened her heart, and when Paul explained to her who Jesus was and how to believe on Him, she responded. Her whole household must have heard also, because they believed and were baptized; and Silas would not have administered the ordinance of baptism if each person had not believed. The point is again illustrated that Paul could have taught Lydia alone. The outcome indicated, however, that he had arranged to meet with her whole household,[8] discipling them into what became the church in her home.

A jail warden, probably a retired Roman army officer, also lived in Philippi. When an earthquake let his prisoners escape, he saw no way out for himself but suicide. Even at that crucial moment Paul did not deal with him alone but saw the potential for evangelizing and discipling the whole family group (Acts 16:30-34).

Paul told the jail warden that salvation was to be found in Jesus Christ and that that salvation was available not only to him by faith but to his whole family as they would believe on Christ. As a result, Paul and Silas, and perhaps Timothy and Luke who might have been nearby, "spoke the word of the Lord to him together with all who were in his house" (Acts 16:32). And all that was sometime after midnight. Even though the hour was late and the time was short, they taught them enough basic theology so that each could make an intelligent, personal decision.

If only the jailer had been discipled, the record would not have included the fact that Paul and his friends spoke the Word of the Lord to the whole household.[9] As a result, the whole family believed and was baptized.

The individuality of their decisions is made clear in verse 34: he "rejoiced greatly, having believed in God *with* his whole household [italics added]." He did not believe *for* them; rather, they believed *with* him.[10] At midnight the father was about to take his own life; by dawn he was the head of a family of God's children.

Crispus, the chief ruler of the synagogue in the city of Corinth, "believed in the Lord with all his household" (Acts 18:8). Again, he did not believe *for* them, but as he took that step, they believed *with* him. It was in the same city that Paul also baptized the *household* of *Stephanas* (1 Cor. 1:16).[11] It was from there, too, that the *household* of *Chloe* later sent word to Paul of

Corinthian church carnality (1 Cor. 1:11).

Paul's practice was to disciple households. Both Jewish and Gentile homes were involved. That emphasis is reflected in Paul's later statement to the church at Corinth that a child with even one Christian parent has a greater likelihood of being saved (1 Cor. 7:14).

It would not be too much to conclude that household evangelism was a primary method of apostolic discipleship. It greatly increased the number of converts *and* the number of new congregations. Christian households frequently became household churches.

Often a detailed record of discipling shows that a whole household was involved, as noted in the cases of Cornelius, Lydia, the jailer, Crispus, and Stephanas. Further, it should be noted that those instances of household evangelism involved a variety of circumstances, countries, and cultures (Roman, Jewish, Greek). Whatever its members' concepts of God were, the family served as the basic unit of communication and decision-making and therefore served as a very appropriate context for discipling.

THE ADVANTAGES OF HOUSEHOLD DISCIPLING

1. Household discipling respects the integrity of the home, moving *with* and not *against* the social unit created by God.

2. Household discipling is usually the most productive method of evangelism. Because the gospel is explained to a whole group at one time, the potential is greater for many to believe than when discipling is limited to individuals.

3. An initial negative response by the family does not negate the value of the method. It is true that families are sometimes resistant, whereas individual family members may be receptive. In such a case, the family must be respected as a social unit and not treated as an adversary, even though it may oppose a believing member.

For instance, in Senegal some young men recently believed on the Lord and were cut off from their Muslim homes. Their lives were threatened. They maintained a respectful attitude, however, attempting to rebuild bridges to the family. They have now been reaccepted and the way is open for them to penetrate their group with the gospel.

4. Household discipling helps to establish a strong group to stand in the

face of opposition and persecution. As families tend to stand together against an outside threat, so a believer in a Christian household is part of a supporting group that stands with him in persecution.

5. Household discipling leads naturally and easily into the establishment of a local church, especially if the household is a large one, as was the case of Nympha (Col. 4:15), Archippus, Philemon (Philem. 1-2), and those at Corinth already mentioned. When the family is not large, it can form a house-church with similar families nearby.

6. Household discipling is often more effective in a village or urban area than individual evangelism is. Pagan households can be attracted to the superior home life of the Christian family.

For example, I recently asked Aaron Francis, an Indian pastor in Durban, South Africa, the most exciting thing happening in his church. Immediately he responded: "Entire Hindu families are coming to Christ!" I asked him what attracted them to the gospel. He told me that Hindu families are often torn apart by greed and arguments. A Christian family invites an entire Hindu family to join them for a day or part of a day. As the members of the Hindu family see the Christian family more and more, they begin to understand the difference Christ makes and often turn to him to be the Savior and Lord of their family. In that practical way, household evangelism reveals Jesus Christ to a whole Hindu family in a way they would never have seen by passing a church building or having a brief individual contact with a Christian.

Perhaps a major weakness of evangelicals today is their failure to disciple whole families, following biblical principles and examples. At the same time, one of the great dangers evangelicals face today is the high potential for the disintegration of the home. The growing erosion of the values and quality of Christian homes needs to be countered by a strong initiative in household discipling—developing in the home healthy, reproducing members of the body of Christ. Not only is this the best defense against family breakdown, it is an overlooked factor for building strong churches.

Household discipling means strong families and growing churches. Household discipling means that family members experience their salvation together and live the Christian life with others. They pray together about common concerns, go through daily experiences, and help one another to apply the Word in daily life. It requires time, trust, and vulnerability—and the work of the Holy Spirit—for each member of the family.

That kind of discipling relates the family to the church in a significant way. It increases the quality of interpersonal relationships within the church. It burdens the father, mother, sons, and daughters to bring their friends to Christ.

Few church families know anything of household discipling. Our churches are missing a tremendous potential for growth in not emphasizing household discipling. As Isaac Simbiri has said, "It is the responsibility of the local church to train and prepare parents to train children in worship and in Bible study. They must be taught how to disciple their children."[12] As that Kenyan leader implies, nothing is automatic in the Christian experience. We must pray and plan and work to be sure that the biblical pattern is followed—evangelism resulting in discipling and discipling resulting in evangelism, and both deeply rooted in the home.

THE IMPORTANCE OF HOUSEHOLD DISCIPLING

1. *The church needs the home to fulfill Christ's command to disciple all nations.* How can a church really do what Christ commanded—disciple all nations? One or two formal services a week are not sufficient, especially when they are primarily designed for worship. Besides, biblical discipling requires close, frequent contact between the discipler and the disciple. That is where the home can work with the church—as part of the church in a smaller unit. The roles of the father, the mother, and older children and the sustained contacts within the family make the home a place that can provide an ideal context for spiritual growth. Whether that training prepares for local or cross-cultural ministry, the home is strategically constituted to bear a heavy load in the process of world evangelization.

2. *The growth of our churches will be largely determined by how well we make disciples.* Church growth in terms of converts and new congregations is directly dependent upon the priority given to it in the home. From His own example, it is evident that Jesus' goal was not "decisions" but disciples. The good news is not just the forgiveness of sins but a whole new life in Christ, a life that the discipler himself must have opportunity to demonstrate in daily life before his disciples.

3. *Christ's own method of building the church by discipling has not been*

superseded. Churches are often concerned with buildings and robes, budgets and rituals. Jesus was primarily concerned with developing men. Discipling is a biblical strategy that cannot be replaced by the multitude of church activities or by the technology of the twentieth century. The foundation of Christian education is discipling, and discipling in the home is one of the most fruitful ways of developing believers, young and old, who would be like Christ in their character, in their concern for the lost, and in their effectiveness in evangelizing them.

4. *Household discipling is the key to fulfilling the pastor's responsibility "for the equipping of the saints for the work of [the ministry]" (Eph. 4:12).* A wise pastor will train leaders of homes, who in turn will help him carry out his work of helping the members of the body to discover their spiritual gifts, develop them, and learn where and how to use them. That kind of activity requires closer and more sustained contact than most pastors can give to individual members of their congregations. Normally, a family member has far more contact with members of his family than with other church members, and certainly more than the pastor or elder has.

A Christian home with free communication and shared spiritual activities holds great potential for the development of the spiritual gifts of its members. By encouraging that kind of activity, the pastor fulfills his own official responsibility and greatly increases his impact on the congregation and the community. That is where the home can work closely with the church, as part of the church in a smaller unit.

THE PLACE OF THE HOME IN JESUS' MINISTRY

Jesus saw the home as an important place in His discipling. He often taught in homes, and usually His disciples were with Him. He used many illustrations from home life—

- The *neighbor* who persistently asked for bread when the family was in bed (Luke 11:5-10)
- The *father* who can be depended on to give his child bread when he asks for it, and not a stone (Luke 11:11-13)
- The *woman* who hid her leaven in the meal (Luke 13:21)
- The *warning* about hiding the light under the bed (Luke 8:16-18)
- *Children* playing wedding and funeral in the marketplace (Luke 7:31-35)

57

- The *little child* set in the midst of the disciples (Luke 18:15-17)

He used those and many more simple, daily pictures to teach eternal truths. I think that for many years afterward fathers and mothers in Galilee probably used those same incidents to teach their families spiritual truths. Jesus saw the home and the ordinary things and events in it as a great opportunity for discipling.

As He prepared to return to His Father, Jesus said to his disciples, "Go therefore and make disciples of all the nations" (Matt. 28:19). He had discipled them and had made them disciplers! That is what the church must do, and the home must be involved in the process. As a church is a family of families, each family, to function as part of the church, must be involved in discipling each of its members. Belonging to the church is not enough. Attending church services is not enough. Knowing God's Word is not enough. Discipling must result in doing. And that kind of doing—discipling—is essential for church growth.

JESUS' DISCIPLING METHOD APPLIED TO HOUSEHOLD DISCIPLING

The example of Jesus, the master discipler, is particularly applicable to household discipling. An insight into His method is found in His prayer on the way to Gethsemane. In the John 17 account we can see five key things Jesus did as He discipled His men:

1. *He chose ordinary laymen (v. 6).* Jesus saw extraordinary potential in ordinary people. He chose, for example, ordinary fishermen using ordinary boats and mending ordinary nets. They were not experts in anything to do with the church. They were not experienced in leadership, or preaching, or evangelism, or writing books. But when they followed Him and committed themselves to His work in their lives, He discipled them. And when He finished with them, they turned the world upside down and wrote eight books in the New Testament.

As we look at the people in our churches and in our homes, we may see ordinary men and women and average young people. Do not be discouraged. Jesus is not discouraged! Those are the kind of people He has chosen to train and use so that they can have the joy of working with the Creator of the universe as He creates new men in Christ Jesus. And He has chosen ordinary people to do it so that God alone will get the glory.

Never underestimate what God can do through the members of your family or the members of your church's families. Household discipling is the key in preparing ordinary people for an extraordinary ministry.

2. *He grounded them in the Word (vv. 8, 14).* Jesus taught them, "If you abide in My word, then you are truly disciples of Mine" (John 8:31). Discipling people in the Word involves three things:

a. *Teaching them.* Most Christians today are ignorant of much of what the Bible teaches. Some need the milk of the Word and some need the meat, but all need to feed!

It is important to teach the Bible systematically in the home. Paul reminded Timothy of how his mother and grandmother had taught him the Holy Scriptures from the time he was a child. The Scriptures not only were "able to give [him] the wisdom that leads to salvation," but they were also "profitable for teaching, for reproof, for correction, for training in righteousness." The child knows what we really think about the Bible by what we do with it in the home (2 Tim. 3:14-17).

b. *Training them for active service.* Two problems may arise as a parent continues to feed a child. If the child does not move around and use what he has taken in, he gets fat. And if he is always fed by the parent, he never learns to feed himself. Those are also dangers when feeding the Word to young believers. But Jesus taught His disciples to move around, to use the truth they had been fed as spiritual energy to minister to others. Had they not gone out after Pentecost, they would have become spiritually fat and useless. Jesus also taught them to feed themselves, to find answers to their questions when He would no longer be there to ask, to search the Scriptures and to feed on them for themselves—the "honey of the Word," as David called it.

Members of our families need to put to use the Word of God they feed on in the home. They need to learn how to use the Word to solve their problems, find guidance and encouragement, and bring others to Jesus. And they need to learn to feed *themselves* on the Word: they need to learn to do it for themselves.

One of the most important things a parent teaches a child is to feed himself. And one of the most important things we can do for our families is to teach each member to meditate on the Word of God each day and apply it to life. For a time, the baby must be fed. Then he learns to feed himself. And then he begins to feed his own children when he has grown up. So it must be in the church. There is no better place for those values and skills to be modeled and taught than in the home.

c. *Developing them into mature Christian leaders.* Day by day, Jesus consistently contributed to their spiritual development. As He taught them to apply scriptural truth in their lives, they developed a hunger and thirst after righteousness and eventually the character that revealed Christ in any kind of situation. Just as Jesus did that by constantly being with His disciples, so parents have an unusual opportunity to build the character of their children in daily experiences.

3. *He both prayed for them and taught them to pray (v. 9).* As Jesus prayed constantly and earnestly *for* His disciples and *with* His disciples, parents need to pray continually *for* and *with* their children. Often we pray for them only when they are sick or in trouble. We need to pray for and with them regularly, asking God to protect them from the evil one, to make them like Jesus, to mature them in the things of the Spirit, and to use them to bring sinners to the Savior. Husbands and wives also need to intercede for each other and pray with each other in those same areas. Members of the family are wonderfully drawn together as their names and needs are mentioned in prayer before the group.

What did the apostles pray for most in the early church? Buildings? Money? Safety? Respect? No. They prayed for boldness—boldness to witness effectively in the midst of strong opposition. Notice that in the prayers recorded in the book of Acts and in Paul's letters (e.g., Acts 4:29 and Eph. 6:18-20). Families need that kind of praying.

4. *He sent them out (v. 18).* Jesus knew that He was sending His men into a hostile world. He protected them (vv. 11-12) by forming them into a team. There is great strength in the unity of the body of Christ. That strength and that unity are experienced by those who are related in a real way to a local church. As one part of the human body protects and strengthens another part, so members of a disciplined, discipled family support each other.

The strength and unity of a group can give believers encouragement to go out together into the hostile world to win men to Christ. What may be difficult and dangerous when done alone can become a strengthening and successful experience when done with other members of the family.

Jesus did not send His disciples out without preparation. He had first taken them with Him as He sought out the lost and told them about the Father. The twelve would listen very carefully for Jesus' response, for instance, as His enemies tried to ensnare Him or as a rich young ruler asked Him how he could inherit eternal life.

Then Jesus sent them out on brief assignments (Matt. 10; Luke 9). As they tried and failed, or perhaps had some success, they always came back to Him. They talked about their experiences and learned. Then, when He went back to heaven, He sent them out on their own in the power of the Spirit. Without that Holy Spirit, that *other Helper,* they would have remained just well-taught fishermen. With Him, they became dynamic disciplers who not only turned the world upside down but who entered into the Master's ministry. They continued all that Jesus began to do and to teach, and they did it in His way.

As those early disciples discovered, the family provides the ideal setting for evangelism. A whole family praying for lost neighbors and friends by name and then reaching out to them, gently and naturally from day to day—that is household discipling, and it causes churches to grow. It brings rejoicing to the heavenly Father, it gives eternal importance to the family, and it brings glory to God. "By this is My Father glorified, that you bear much fruit" (John 15:8). Churches grow when families *grow*—and *go* to win the lost.

Discussion Questions

1. Define *household discipling*. Is it a viable concept? Discuss its biblical roots. In each case, what was involved?
2. Tell why the family serves as an appropriate context for discipling.
3. In what ways is household discipling important to church growth?
4. How is the example of Jesus, the master discipler, particularly applicable to household discipling?

1. George W. Peters, *Saturation Evangelism* (Grand Rapids: Zondervan, 1976), p. 149.
2. Ibid.
3. "He and his whole household came to believe"—W. F. Arndt and F. W. Gingrich,

A Greek-English Lexicon of the New Testament (Chicago: U. of Chicago Press, 1957), p. 560.
4. Arndt and Gingrich, p. 563.
5. That does not detract from the concept of the integrity of the family. It was because whole families were involved that the home was the most appropriate place for the event. See the parallel of the Passover observance.
6. F. F. Bruce, *The Book of Acts* (Grand Rapids: Eerdmans, 1973), p. 81. See also Arndt and Gingrich, p. 563.
7. Although the context emphasizes a ministry in homes in contrast to a public ministry, the construction is the same as that of Acts 2:46 and would refer to the family within the house.
8. Bruce comments: "When she was baptized, together with her household (presumably her servants and other dependents) . . ." (Bruce, p. 391).
9. Arndt and Gingrich cite that reference as an illustration of *oikos*, "household, family."
10. Greek, "together with." So also in Acts 18:8 below.
11. Arndt and Gingrich: "Stephanas and his family," (p. 563).
12. Isaac Simbiri, Christian Education Coordinator of the Africa Inland Church in Kenya. Stated in a paper read at the Third Triennial General Assembly of the Association of Evangelicals of Africa and Madagascar, August 3-10, 1977, at Bouake, Ivory Coast.

Leadership for the Church

3

New Testament Guidelines for Starting and Organizing Local Churches

Vergil Gerber

The church in New Testament perspective is neither incidental nor accidental. Establishing the goal toward which all theological education is directed, Jesus enunciates with incisive language: "I will build My church; and the gates of Hades shall not overpower it" (Matt. 16:18). Fulfillment of the evangelistic mandate, therefore, is measured in terms of the church (Matt. 28:19-20).

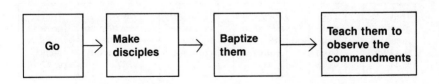

Theological education falls short of its objective unless it relates individuals to the local community of the redeemed. "To be an effective Christian it is not enough to be an individual believer," Elton Trueblood asserts. "Men are never really effective unless they share in some kind of group reality. Inadequate as the fellowship of the church may be in many generations, including our own, there is not the slightest chance of Christian vitality without it. New life normally arises from inside,"[1] Using the biblical metaphor of fire, Trueblood further elucidates:

> Much of the uniqueness of Christianity, in its original emergence, consisted of the fact that simple people could be amazingly powerful when they were members one of another. As everyone knows, it is almost impossible to create a fire with one log, even if it is a sound one, while several poor logs may make an excellent fire if they stay together as they burn. The miracle of the early church was that of poor sticks making a grand conflagration.[2]

Trueblood adds the following as well:

> Evangelism occurs when people are so enkindled by contact with the central fire of Christ that they, in turn, set others on fire. The only adequate evidence that anything is on fire is the pragmatic evidence that other fires are started by it. A fire that does not spread must eventually go out! This is the point of Emil Brunner's dictum that "the church exists by mission as fire exists by burning." A person who claims to have a religious experience yet makes no effort to share or to extend it, has not really entered into Christ's Company at all. In short, an unevangelistic or unmissionary Christianity is a contradiction in terms.[3]

So the church is both the goal and the agent of dynamic reproduction. On the day of Pentecost, the first church in Jerusalem added 3,000 to its embryonic fellowship of 120 members. The new group in turn reached out into the metropolitan community, gaining favor with people. And day after day the Lord added to their number people who were being saved (Acts 2).[4]

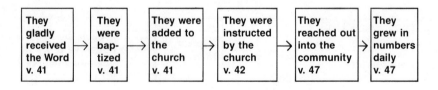

| They gladly received the Word v. 41 | They were baptized v. 41 | They were added to the church v. 41 | They were instructed by the church v. 42 | They reached out into the community v. 47 | They grew in numbers daily v. 47 |

The early *koinonia* was much more than a local fellowship as an end in itself. The root meaning of the Greek word is "to have in common, to share with others." Barnabas and Paul received the right hand of fellowship *(koinonias)* at Jerusalem *in order that*[5] they might go to the nations (Gal. 2:9). It is in that missionary dimension that Beyerhaus and Lefever define the church as being "at one and the same time the community of the redeemed and the redeeming community."[6]

The mission to reproduce herself in every nation is the dominating motif of the book of Acts—the acts of the early church. Her spiritual dynamic is the *dunamis*[7] of Pentecost. Just as the splitting of the atom and the explosion of power that resulted set off a chain reaction that shook the world of the twentieth century and released a nuclear energy hitherto unknown, so in striking parallel the explosion of power on the Day of Pentecost had set off a chain reaction that shook the world of the first century and released a spiritual energy hitherto unknown. That dynamic quality in the Person of the Holy Spirit is promised to the disciples for the explicit purpose of multiplying nuclear cells around the world (Acts 1:8).

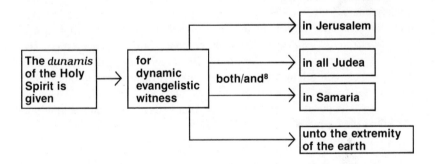

As J. B. Phillips writes in the preface to his translation of Acts,

> No one can read this book without being convinced that there is Someone here at work besides mere human beings. The newborn church, as vulnerable as any human child, having neither money, influence nor power in the ordinary sense, is setting forth joyfully and courageously to win the pagan world for God through Christ. These men did not make acts of faith, they believed; they did not

say their prayers, they really prayed. They did not hold conferences on psychosomatic medicine, they simply healed the sick. Consequently it is a matter of sober historical fact that never before has any small body of ordinary people so moved the world that their enemies could say, with tears of rage in their eyes, that these men have turned the world upside down! [Acts 17:6][9]

As Harry R. Boer says, "The Great Commission derives its meaning and power wholly and exclusively from the Pentecost event."[10] Boer goes on to say, "Restlessly the Spirit drives the Church to witness, and continually churches rise out of witness."[11] Dynamic, living cells multiply into hundreds of congregations in Asia, Europe, Africa, and around the world. The book of Acts is the historical record of first-century church multiplication through missionary witness in the power of the Holy Spirit.

There are two parallel truths that, if properly understood, lay the foundation for starting and organizing local churches overseas:

1. *Men cannot produce the church.* Only God can produce the church, for the church is the life of God in action. All life originates with God. Its unique characteristic is its reproductive quality. It cannot be self-contained. Spiritual reproduction, whether on the individual or collective level, is intrinsically and uniquely the work of the Holy Spirit. Neither methods nor men, however good, can reproduce the life of the church. That is the Spirit's ministry.

2. *Men are God's method.* Although men are wholly dependent upon the Spirit for the reproduction of the life of the church, in paradoxical contrast God has made Himself wholly dependent upon men for the building of His church. "God's methods are men, and we are the men!" Melvin Hodges affirms. "Methods are no better than the men behind them; and men are no better than their contact with God."[12] Edgar A. Guest rightly penned it:

God builds no churches. By His plan
That labor has been left to man.
No spires miraculously arise;
No little mission from the skies
Falls on the bleak and barren place
To be a source of strength and grace.
The humblest church demands its price
In human toil and sacrifice.
Men call the church the House of God,

Toward which the toil-stained pilgrims trod
In search of strength and rest and hope,
As blindly through life's mist they grope.
And there God dwells, but it is man
Who builds that house and draws its plan;
Pays for mortar and the stone
That none need seek for God alone.
The humblest spire in mortal ken
Where God abides was built by men.
And if the church is still to grow,
Is still the light of hope to throw
Across the valley of despair,
Men still must build God's House of Prayer.
God sends no churches from the skies.
Out of our hearts must they arise.[13]

What Guest is saying is: *There is no such thing as an "instant church."* In this twentieth century, when everything comes in instant "how to do it" packages that guarantee maximum results at minimum effort, churches are still born out of travail of soul. No miracle drug or promotional stimulant can eliminate the hard labor of bringing churches into existence. Even after two thousand years of Christian experience and evangelistic know-how in the ecclesiastical science of church birth, there are still no easy formulas or simple how-to-do-it package plans for church reproduction. Winston Churchill's pugent words *"blood, sweat, and tears"* serve to remind us that the church too is born of blood, sweat, and tears—the blood of Christ, the sweat of discipleship, and the tears of prevailing prayer.

Yet although God has left it to men to build His church, He has not left to trial and error the construction of that church. *Too often we start with missionary activity rather than with the missionary objective. We recruit volunteer workers rather than craftsmen. We equip them with scaffolds and tools and material resources. And we send them out. But we neglect to provide them with the necessary know-how for building or with a clearly defined plan for starting and organizing churches overseas—as if churches were of secondary importance, a sort of by-product of Christian mission.* For any other career we require specialized training. What would happen if we required a major in church extension and a year's internship in church planting before graduating missionaries or sending them to the field? "It is highly important," says T. Stanley Soltau, "that missionary candidates be well acquainted with the goal of mission work in terms of an indigenous church and with the New Testament principles by which this goal can be attained."[14]

Building means planning. No one would think of constructing a building without a well-defined plan to follow. It is not enough to provide materials and hire workmen. A building starts with an architect's concept of the end result to be achieved. Once that objective is agreed upon, a careful plan of construction is drawn up. That blueprint is then carried out in detail by experienced laborers. All three parts are vital if the project is to be a success.

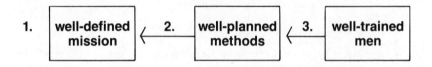

1. well-defined mission ← 2. well-planned methods ← 3. well-trained men

The three parts come through with remarkable clarity in the pages of New Testament history. Robert Coleman refers to that biblical blueprint as "the master plan of evangelism."[15] What he sees in the pattern laid down by our Lord and His early followers is a detailed blueprint for numerical multiplication of visible, local fellowships in every nation. Let us look at it:

1. WELL-DEFINED MISSION

On the Day of Pentecost (Acts 2) we see a responsible church growing out of witness. Filled with the Holy Spirit, the first Christians began to speak—not in unintelligible babble but in effective communication (vv. 4-11). And men from every nation under heaven received their witness (v. 5). The result: 3000 were baptized and added to the Jerusalem fellowship (v. 41). Many others carried the seeds of the church to foreign soil.

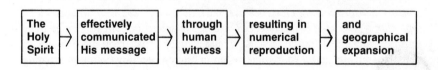

The Holy Spirit → effectively communicated His message → through human witness → resulting in numerical reproduction → and geographical expansion

What clearly emerges is a newborn church with all the characteristics of what Beyerhaus and Lefever call "responsible selfhood."[16] From the church's inception, individual and corporate responsibility can be seen in the following:

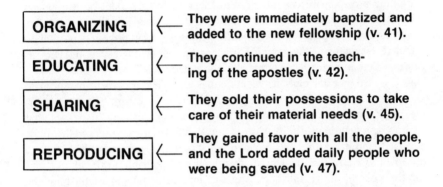

ORGANIZING	←	**They were immediately baptized and added to the new fellowship (v. 41).**
EDUCATING	←	**They continued in the teaching of the apostles (v. 42).**
SHARING	←	**They sold their possessions to take care of their material needs (v. 45).**
REPRODUCING	←	**They gained favor with all the people, and the Lord added daily people who were being saved (v. 47).**

The self-determining and self-continuing nature of the Jerusalem church gives striking evidence of its well-defined mission. Across the pages of the Pentecost event could well be written: "Mission Accomplished!"

At the same time, the church's mission was yet to be accomplished. As Alexander McLeish points out in his Princeton lectures, the establishing of a responsible church is not only central to the existence of the faith but to its proclamation to the world. "The object of its existence is to expand its fellowship to all nations."[17] He views the calling into being of the new fellowship as the agent for worldwide missionary purpose. Turning the pages of the historic blueprint we see the fulfillment of that purpose in churches being reproduced in Judea, Galilee, Samaria, and most of the then-known world. How was it accomplished? What specific methods produced that phenomenal first-century expansion? For an answer, we follow the pattern laid down by the greatest of all New Testament missionaries, the apostle Paul.

2. WELL-PLANNED METHODS

Paul's methods were directly related to his predetermined mission. All of his missionary activity contributed to that end goal. "His was no vague effort to meet universal need which so often inspires what we loosely call 'evangelism,' " says McLeish.[18] He concentrated on the creation and care of churches.

Let us begin with his relationship to the Antioch church. Paul started by becoming a responsible member (Acts 13:1). As a Christian, he recognized that he was responsible *to* the church and *for* the church. *Responsible churches are made up of responsible members.* That principle is vital to effective evangelism. Accepting Christ as Savior means accepting Him as Lord. And that means responsible church-relatedness. That "cost of discipleship," as Bonhoeffer calls it, stands out in the New Testament blueprint in sharp relief against the easy believism of modern evangelism. "Cheap grace is the deadly enemy of the church," says Bonhoeffer.[19] He also says that "Christianity without discipleship is always Christianity without Christ."[20] The first step in starting and organizing local churches overseas is to "make disciples" (Matt. 28:19)—Christians who are responsible to the church and for the church. If we fail here, we will inevitably fail in establishing the church.

Paul, along with Barnabas and others, spent eleven years developing the responsible selfhood of the Antioch church. From the beginning Paul recognized the centrality and autonomy of the local fellowship. He placed himself under its direction and discipline. It was to the *church* that the Spirit finally spoke: "Set apart for Me Barnabas and Saul for the work to which I have called them" (Acts 13:2). It was *the church* that sent them forth on their first missionary journey. It was to *the church* that they returned to report (Acts 14:27). Here then is a principle of interresponsibility: the missionary responsible to the church and the church responsible for the missionary.

Furthermore, the church is both independent and interdependent. Paul and Barnabas were sent by the church at Antioch to the Jerusalem church to report on their missionary work. Hearing the report, the latter took official action on the report, making certain recommendations that had far-reaching effect on the founding of new churches in other places (Acts 15:19-29). McLeish observes that "this acknowledgment of the church at every stage of his work has, for a man of St. Paul's independence of mind, a very special significance for us."[21] Those two principles of interrelationship stand out with clarity:

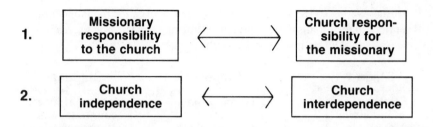

Paul's carefully planned methods for starting and organizing churches
concentrated on the population centers: Iconium, Lystra, Derbe, Antioch,
Pisidia, Pamphylia, Perga, Attalia (Acts 14). *The cities were his target.* He
went where the greatest number of people were. At times he preached in the
synagogues, at other times in the marketplace or the open air. Sometimes he
concentrated on individuals, at other times on the masses. But his strategy was
always to concentrate on the areas of greatest potential for church growth.
Although preaching and witnessing planted the seed, they were never an end
in themselves. They were always followed by in-depth instruction with the
view to making responsible disciples (Acts 14:21).[22] Paul never seemed hur-
ried. He took the time needed to develop responsible converts into a responsible fellowship. In Corinth he spent a whole year and a half (Acts 18:11). In
Ephesus he needed three years (Acts 20:31). In Rome he stayed two years.
When any church was sufficiently mature, he encouraged the group to appoint
leaders *(presbyteros),* committed the newly organized church to the Lord in
prayer, and moved on to another place (Acts 14:23).

*The simplicity of church government in New Testament practice is not
accidental.* As J. B. Phillips says, "This surely is the church as it was meant
to be. It is vigorous and flexible, for these are the days before it ever became
fat and short of breath through prosperity, or muscle bound by over organization."[23] Paul clearly outlined for Timothy, a young church planter and convert
of his in whom he had invested considerable time and training, the qualifications necessary for the two offices of the church—bishop-elder-pastor and
deacon (1 Tim. 3:1-13).[24] The need for those offices arose as a result of the
phenomenal growth of the church at Jerusalem and its resultant problem (Acts
6:1-7).

Gustav Warneck (1834-1910), who has often been called the founder of the scientific study of missionary principles, distinguishes *three stages* in the process of building a responsible church[25]:

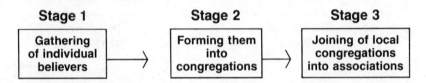

Stage 1		Stage 2		Stage 3
Gathering of individual believers	→	Forming them into congregations	→	Joining of local congregations into associations

That is in keeping with the principle of interrelationship we observed in the Antioch and Jerusalem churches—that is, the early fellowships were interdependent.

Although many twentieth-century missionaries look for a building as the first step in the development of a church, even before the preaching of the gospel, the New Testament lays little or no stress upon a building as the necessary means to the formation of a church. Erroneously we speak today of "the church on Main and Walnut streets." But the New Testament leaves no room for such interpretation. The Greek word literally means "called out ones," and it is used in the Scriptures to denote the assembling of believers together in a certain place or to designate a specific fellowship of believers in a particular place. Hence we read of "the church of the Thessalonians" (1 Thess. 1:1) or the church meeting in the house of Nympha (Col. 4:15). It is true that Paul often began his initial efforts preaching at the local synagogue of the Jews, but a synagogue is never considered a church in the New Testament. For many years the early believers met in homes and never possessed any special buildings for their gatherings (Rom. 16:5; 1 Cor. 16:19; Col. 4:15; Philem. 2).

"There is no clear example of a separate building set apart for Christian worship within the limits of the Roman empire before the third century."[26] Paul concentrated his efforts not on buildings but on men. Men are God's method.

3. WELL-TRAINED MEN

"It all started by Jesus' calling a few men to follow Him. . . . His concern was not with programs to reach the multitudes, but with men whom the multitudes would follow. Remarkable as it may seem, Jesus started to gather these men before He ever organized an evangelistic campaign or even preached a sermon in public. . . . The initial objectives of Jesus' plan was to enlist men who could bear witness to His life and carry on His work after He returned to the Father."[27]

Jesus' selection of disciples was done with the utmost care. Prior to the selection of the twelve He spent all night in prayer (Luke 6:12-16). Those men at first do not impress us as being outstanding church leaders, but what is evident is their willingness to learn. And Jesus concentrated His teaching on those few. "Here is the wisdom of His method . . . the fundamental principle of concentration on those He intended to use. . . . The necessity is apparent not only to select a few laymen, but to keep the group small enough to be able to work effectively with them."[28]

As we have already noted, Paul likewise concentrated on potential leaders (Timothy, John, Mark, Aquila and Priscilla, Philemon, etc.). In writing to Timothy he underlined "and the things which you have heard from me in the presence of many witnesses, these entrust to faithful men, who will be able to teach others also" (2 Tim. 2:2). Here is the "each one teach one" philosophy of missions: making reproducing Christians who in turn will make other reproducing Christians. Here is the mathematical solution to world evangelism—multiplication rather than simple addition.

Although great stress today is laid on money and methods, men are still God's means for reproducing responsible churches. "We can study methods of church growth and write books about indigenous church principles, all of which is well and good; but we will never have anything like New Testament churches and New Testament growth until we get something like New Testament men with New Testament experience. I do not know how this affects you, but it challenges me to the depths of my being. God's methods are men, and we are the men!"[29]

Discussion Questions

1. How is the church both the goal and the agent of dynamic reproduction? How does the meaning of the Greek word *koinonia* substantiate that?

2. Explain the biblical paradox that states, on the one hand, that men are wholly dependent upon God for the building of His church and, on the other hand, that God has made Himself wholly dependent upon men for its accomplishment.
3. State in your own terms the principle of interrelatedness of churches in the New Testament—that is, their independence and interdependence. Discuss Warneck's stages in the process of building a responsible church.

1. Elton Trueblood, *The Company of the Committed* (New York: Harper & Row, 1961), p. 21.
2. Elton Trueblood, *The Incendiary Fellowship* (New York: Harper & Row, 1967). p. 107.
3. Ibid., p. 111.
4. Notice the use of the present participle *sozomenous* (were being saved) in the original text (v. 47).
5. A purpose clause introduced by the preposition *hina*.
6. Peter Beyerhaus and Henry Lefever, *The Responsible Church and the Foreign Mission* (Grand Rapids: Eerdmans, 1964), p. 110.
7. English derivatives: *dynamite, dynamic*.
8. Note that it is "both/and," not "either/or."
9. J. B. Phillips, *The Young Church in Action* (New York: Macmillan, 1955), p. vii.
10. Harry R. Boer, *Pentecost and Missions* (Grand Rapids: Eerdmans, 1961), p. 47.
11. Ibid., p. 161.
12. Donald McGavran, *Church Growth and Christian Mission* (New York: Harper & Row, 1965), p. 32.
13. Edgar A. Guest, "On Church Building," in *The Collected Verse of Edgar A. Guest* (Chicago: Reilly and Lee, 1934), pp. 662-63. Reprinted from *The Collected Verse of Edgar A. Guest,* © 1934 with the permission of Contemporary Books, Inc., Chicago.
14. T. Stanley Soltau, *Missions at the Crossroads* (Wheaton, Ill.: VanKampen, 1954), pp. 18-19.
15. Robert E. Coleman, *The Master Plan of Evangelism* (Old Tappan, N.J.: Revell, 1963).
16. Beyerhaus and Lefever, p. 21.
17. Alexander McLeish, *Objective and Method in Christian Expansion* (London: World Dominion, 1952), p. 11.
18. Ibid., p. 8.

19. Dietrich Bonhoeffer, *The Cost of Discipleship* (New York: Macmillan, 1967), p. 45.
20. Ibid., p. 64.
21. McLeish, p. 8.
22. Note that the Greek participle is *matheteusantes* (had made disciples) not *didaskontes* (had taught).
23. Phillips, p. vii.
24. For *bishop-elder-pastor,* see also Acts 20:17, 28 and 1 Peter 5:1-3. The Greek words used in these verses give a threefold picture of the office and the officeholder: as bishop he is the overseer of the affairs of the church; as elder he is the respected leader of the congregation; as pastor he is the spiritual caretaker of the flock. (See H. E. Dana, *A Manual of Ecclesiology,* 2d ed. rev. in collaboration with L. M. Sipes [Kansas City: Central Seminary Press, 1944], pp. 92-93.)

    "The origin of the office of *Deacon* is usually ascribed to Acts 6:1-6. . . .The verb translated 'serve' is from the same root as the noun translated 'deacon' " (Dana, pp. 88-89).
25. Beyerhaus and Lefever, p. 49.
26. J. B. Lightfoot, *St. Paul's Epistle to the Philippians* (London and Cambridge: Macmillan, 1869), p. 241.
27. Coleman, p. 21.
28. Ibid., p. 24.
29. Melvin Hodges in McGavran, p. 32.

4

Sharpening the Focus:
Theological Education in Guatemala

A. Clark Scanlon

World trends and events combine to emphasize the sobering knowledge of the urgency of the Christian missionary's task. The much publicized population explosion alone demands that theological education be conducted wisely. Knowing that the ultimate will of a compassionate God is that He wants all men everywhere to come to Him through Jesus Christ (2 Pet. 3:9) and that the establishing of His church in every part of the world is central to that evangelistic purpose, the missionary—particularly the one involved in leadership training—must resharpen his focus on winning large numbers of those lost multitudes.

If lostness means anything, the missionary must be shaken out of any complacency that might allow him the luxury of an ivory-tower approach. He is involved in the front-line battle, where the souls of men are at stake. The destiny of countless lives is related to the preparation, the orientation, and the spirit he gives to those whom he has the privilege and responsibility to train.

The principles of theological education projected in this study have been tested against the experience of five major denominations and missions work-

A. CLARK SCANLON (Th.D., Southwestern Baptist Theological Seminary) serves in Guatemala with the Southern Baptist Foreign Mission Board as field representative for Middle America. For five years Dr. Scanlon was president of the Guatemalan Baptist Theological Seminary.

ing in the country of Guatemala, Central America: the Central American Mission, the Presbyterian Synod of Guatemala, the Assemblies of God, the Friends, and the Convention of Baptist Churches of Guatemala. Each of those denominations or associations of churches has at least doubled its membership in the last ten years and provides concrete examples of church growth through theological education that can be used for analysis and evaluation. That those schools represent the training program of churches with a total membership of more than 70,000 indicates that they are growing churches. The mailing list of the American Bible Society in 1980 reveals 3,500 to 4,000 evangelical churches in Guatemala. Their theological training programs have a number of discernible features in common. Those programs are evaluated not on the basis of the strengths and weaknesses of individual schools but with specific reference to the growth potential of their denominations. Theological education by extension, pioneered by the Presbyterians, has had wide use in each of the groups.

FACTORS FAVORABLE TO GROWTH

1. CONSERVATIVE THEOLOGY

Although there is much difference in ecclesiastical organization, methods of work, and emphasis on individual section of doctrine, there is a remarkable unity among missionaries and nationals on cardinal doctrines. Those include the lostness of man, the sufficiency of Jesus Christ, the authority of the Word of God, and the obligation to evangelize. The presentation of the divine Christ as the adequate Lord for each man's life gives the ring of authority to preaching and teaching. That conviction becomes an invaluable spiritual arm in seeking the kind of growth witnessed in the book of Acts.

2. EMPHASIS ON EVANGELISM

Each of the theological institutions under study has both classes in evangelism and practical field work. Expansion is not only welcomed, it is actively sought. Evangelism is not a course to be taught, it is a life to be lived.

In the Baptist Theological Seminary, Tuesday is testimony day. The students report their experiences in witnessing and soul-winning from the previous week. Other institutions have similar days. The Central American Bible

Institute (Central American Mission International) observes days of prayer periodically to help develop a burden for the lost as well as to invoke divine aid. Such an environment is conducive to optimum learning of methods of church growth.

3. PRACTICAL WORK OF STUDENTS

Students of those schools do many kinds of practical work, but all such work forms a standard part of their training. Students from the Assembly of God Central Bible Institute and the Baptist Theological Seminary are often pastors while in school. Those who do not pastor go to churches and preaching points to seek the expansion of the Kingdom of God. The Assemblies of God students are in the field eight months of the year and in school four. At some time during the four-year course of study, the students of the Baptist Theological Seminary of Guatemala must spend a year of practice in the field.

Students at Central American Bible Institute and Robinson Bible Institute (also CAM International) have a variety of tasks. One special feature is the evangelism classes for children. Part of the young women's work in Robinson Bible Institute includes teaching a Bible class in the local government high school. *Practical evangelism is a necessary part of any program to train men in planting churches.* The vast majority of the churches of the Central American Mission in the Lake Atitlán, Sololá, and Chimaltenango region are results of practical work by students of the Robinson Bible Institute.

4. TEACHERS WITH COMPASSIONATE HEARTS

Most of the teachers interviewed reflected a compassionate concern for the winning of the lost. That spirit, spread by contagion, is one of the most valuable assets of the schools. Some schools have found that inviting warm-hearted pastors to serve as teachers and chapel speakers spreads the spirit of expectancy and evangelistic outreach among the students. The seeking attitude develops as the student catches fire from the teacher.

5. TRAINING BY ASSOCIATION

Jesus took His fishermen disciples with Him *on the job* in order to teach them how to win people. Paul used the same method when he took Timothy and Silas with him. They became spiritual interns, learning church building from the greatest missionary.

In training by association, the student can be assigned to a pastor successful in church growth. The student learns from practical experience and observation. In other cases a missionary with a gift of evangelism fills the role of the practical teacher. For example, two students of the Baptist Theological Seminary spent a year of practical work beside the missionary known to be the finest soul-winner of his mission. During that time both young men gained great ability as winners of men. As a result of their work, new worshiping groups that will grow into churches sprang up like spring wheat.

Another missionary took laymen with him on trips to churches and preaching points. During the long hours of travel, he told them his goals of winning large populations to Christ. He talked about his own experiences in soul-winning and emphasized the laymen's responsibility in the practice. As a direct result, new emphases on the outreach of churches became evident. New preaching points were opened! Those men became leaders in their local churches and are becoming sensitive to spiritual need in other areas. Training by association is a valuable asset to the work and should be developed and expanded.

6. INCORPORATION OF GUATEMALAN LEADERSHIP

Each of the seminaries, institutes, and Bible schools has recognized that tomorrow's leaders will be Guatemalans. That national point of view can help prevent the wholesale importation of foreign methods. Every effort should be made to secure nationals who are capable in the course they teach. As teachers interpret the gospel in their own national thought forms and cultural patterns, they substitute *planting* for *transplanting*. Those schools have recognized the importance and urgency of having Guatemalans on the faculty and in their administration and have made a permanent and growing place for them.

7. RECOGNITION OF WEB RELATIONSHIPS

In several towns the principle of seeking new converts along the lines of family relationships has been recognized and followed. The Central American Mission church in the town of Patzún has a membership of over six hundred among the Cakchiquel Indians of that region. The majority of those members are kinsmen and have sought each other on that basis.

In the town of San Pedro La Laguna on Lake Atitlán some 40 percent of the town of five thousand are evangelical Christians and members of the Central American Mission, Baptist, Pentecostal, and interdenominational churches. In many cases entire families of a score or more are members of one of those churches.

The nearby town of Santiago, Atitlán, shows how the web of relationships influences church growth. The Central American Mission, the Baptist, the Assemblies of God, and other churches work in the town. A large portion of the membership of the Central American Mission church is related to the Mendoza family. A sizable portion of the Baptist church members comes from the Ramirez family. In another Baptist church, the pastor estimates that 171 persons come from three extended families. The Pentecostals come from still another family. During the late sixties one young pastor adopted the suggestion of his former teacher to work along family lines. The church experienced a marked increase in membership.

FACTORS NOT FAVORABLE TO GROWTH

A special kind of humility is required to examine one's cherished program and ask, Is this the best way to win people and establish churches for Christ? The subsequent question is even more difficult: Are our churches multiplying at the rate of 100 percent or 200 percent per decade, and is that commensurate with the white fields into which God sends us? Are we rejoicing in 80 percent growth per decade, when 300 percent is possible? Which factors that retard growth are at work in our training program? What can we do about it?

1. TREATING THEOLOGICAL EDUCATION AS AN END IN ITSELF

A subtle danger to church expansion through pastoral training must be combated. The leaders of an institution may become interested in "bettering" the school, in "raising its standards." Better buildings, more efficient answering of examination questions, better presentation of messages and church programs by cultured ministers may become both criteria and goals. When such a process begins, the theological training institution has become an end in itself.

The plumbline must be: Are these graduates adapting themselves to the local people whom they understand and with whom they can work to produce soul-winning churches? *The end result of a training program must be the planting and expanding of churches.* Those churches must be grounded in the fundamental doctrines of the faith. An evangelistic emphasis will insure growth in other areas of the Christian life.

If the training is producing other than soul-winning, church-building graduates, it is missing its mark. A good measuring stick is found in the teacher himself, missionary or national. How often does he engage in soul-winning and pushing into new areas? If the load of activities becomes too heavy for that practice, the load is just too heavy! The teacher's priorities need reevaluation.

2. FAILURE TO UNDERSTAND PEOPLES

Peoples, a plural word, here refers to language groups, tribes, clans, kindreds—the more or less homogeneous subgroups found within a population. Members of a specific People tend to intermarry, to dress similarly, and to make changes as a group. In a city, a people may be a foreign group that has moved into a country and maintains itself somewhat apart, observing the customs of the old country.

In Guatemala missionaries need to study the history and cultural anthropology of indigenous groups. If more missionaries had the anthropological understanding of the Wycliffe Translators, they would discern many more responsive tribes. That understanding might result in a turning to Christ of great numbers. Such comprehension will not inevitably lead to a people movement to Christ. It only offers a tool to the man who is motivated by the love of Christ, empowered by the Spirit of Christ, and aggressive in his presentation of Christ. As he uses that tool, he may witness a great ingathering.

3. FAILURE TO PROJECT AN OVERALL STRATEGY

The Holy Spirit is the master planner. He leads men out to look for lost sheep. He is the giver of church growth. At the same time, men's failure to cooperate with the plans and purposes of God's Spirit may lead to scanty results. Theological education must be sensitive to God's will for the salvation of multitudes. Plans for a liberation of those peoples through great expansion of evangelical churches must be told to the students. The Holy Spirit has plans for the redemption of Guatemala. Theological education's high calling is to communicate them to the students and to prepare the students to expect the Holy Spirit's continued guidance as they attempt great things for God.

Important questions must be answered: In which direction does greatest responsiveness present itself? Are there responsive areas to which we have not given sufficient attention? Which tribes or clans are most ready to march out of Egypt? Is the method currently employed one that will accelerate the rate of growth? Or will it actually decelerate it?

A wise strategy insures optimum conservation of results. A good plan for the utilization, training, and involvement of new converts can help safeguard continuing growth. A lack of vision and imagination may characterize a work that has enjoyed success in times past.

4. LACK OF STATISTICS NECESSARY FOR CAREFUL MEASUREMENT OF GROWTH

The lack of essential statistics, a weakness fairly universal among the national denominational entities studied, should be corrected to permit more fruitful and intelligent planning for the future. It is not enough to know that one is growing; the areas of growth must be examined also. The factors that influence growth ought to be studied. The knowledge gained from such investigation becomes extremely useful in teaching students what procedure has met with success in their own environment.

Statistics are valuable measuring sticks with which to evaluate a determined project. Does a school actually contribute to the growth of the churches in the region? Over a period of several years will areas where schools are located show consistently greater growth than others where they are not present? True statistics can be an excellent antidote to self-hypnosis. They bring missions and churches face-to-face with the reality of a situation.

5. EMPHASIS ON YOUNG MEN AND WOMEN ONLY

More closely related to the theological institution itself stands a danger that is both subtle and difficult to remedy. Following the traditional pattern in the United States, where the mature man entering the ministry is the exception rather than the rule, the training of only young people for the ministry has been accepted in Guatemala as axiomatic. Young people seem to be the only ones God calls to the ministry. When someone has entered the ministry later in life to become an outstanding pastor, he is regarded as a notable exception.

Young people should continue to be enlisted, but there should be increasing provision for the training of family men who feel the call of God to dedicate themselves to His work. Those men cannot meet the same kind of training schedule that young, unattached people can. On the other hand, their maturity, insight, and ability to sustain themselves frequently enables them to become reliable pastors.

Young men and women may be trained away from their environment. Realization that older men in the congregations—the natural leaders—should be trained may upset some cherished plan of the theological institution. However, the Assemblies of God have been strong in carrying out this principle. Shorter terms may have to be offered. The TEE of the Presbyterians, the Paul Bell Theological Institute of the Baptists, and the Central American Mission's night classes take that principle into account. Classes may have to be taught nearer the homes of church leaders in order to reach those valuable members of the church.

6. PRIMARY EMPHASIS ON THE INTELLECTUAL

Most of the entrance requirements have to do with intellectual achievements. The ideal of pietistic education that the heart increases in compassion as the head grows in knowledge is a good corrective. "Raising the standards" or "bettering the school" must be always in terms of the end product sought. For theological education, that product is men and women trained to extend the Kingdom of God in their native land. Discipleship, not mere intellectual training, is the criterion. No amount of intellectual training can substitute for spiritual power. The constant exercise of spiritual gifts must accompany all intellectual training. Christlike compassion for the lost should be the goal of every teacher for his students.

7. SUBSIDY A DANGER

All the institutions studied receive a measure of subsidy. Although their work would be severely limited without the subsidy, two dangers must be prevented: (1) the raising of the standard of living to the point where a student is no longer content to work among his own people, and (2) the provision of scholarships that will for all future years orient the student toward the expectation of mission support. Tragic cases have occurred when a man's manner of living and tastes "progressed" to the point at which he was no longer content to work among his own people. A training institution must produce better Guatemalan ministers! If a man has advanced himself but has lost the feeling of solidarity with his own family and friends, a serious question mark must be placed on that school's training program.

A scholarship program may set the pattern for a highly trained, paid ministry that can neither reach nor be supported by the churches. Almost without exception, a high standard of living requires subsidy to meet it. As another side effect, such a standard may discourage lay witnessing. The logic is as follows: witnessing is something for which one must be well paid. If not, there is no witnessing.

Melvin Hodges points out four dangers to which such a worker may be subject. (1) He may have difficulty in leading the national church. (2) He may lack initiative. (3) He may encounter difficulty in adapting himself to the humble living conditions of his field of service. (4) He may continue to look to the missionary rather than to God to care for his financial needs.[1]

8. FAILURE TO USE QUALIFIED EXPERTS IN EVANGELISM AND CHURCH GROWTH

By what virtue, by what right does a leader stand before a class in evangelism or missions or church expansion? Is it because his turn came to teach that subject? Is it because he has a degree, or because he received an excellent rating in that subject in a United States seminary? The criterion must be that the man that teaches evangelism or church growth or missions knows by personal experience about church growth in the populations to which the students go. A fruitful practice in lay-training institutes sponsored by the Guatemalan Baptist Seminary includes inviting the pastor who has had the greatest amount of growth each year to teach evangelism in those short courses. His teaching manner may not be the most polished available, but his experience is invaluable. Many such men are available but unrecognized.

9. DISCOURAGEMENT OF LAY WITNESSING THROUGH THE CREATION OF A PROFESSIONAL CLASS

In a meeting of church leaders, the head of a theological institution voiced concern over the professionalism that develops in ministers who have had the advantages of training. Such professionalism creates laymen lethargical in their witnessing. A corrective is the emphasis that a call to the ministry is a call to service. Roman Catholicism with its hard and fast distinction between laity and clergy has helped create even in Protestants in Latin America the feeling that only the minister can preach, witness, or teach.

10. TRANSPLANTING OF TRADITIONAL PATTERNS

One final danger to church growth to be found in theological education must be spotlighted. It may be the greatest of the many enemies of church expansion through the indigenous church. In another sense, it is the summary of all the other problems. It occurs in curriculum, program, and outlook. This unfavorable factor might be summarized as making the pastoral-training institution largely a copy of older institutions in the United States or Europe.

McGavran's phrase for the above-mentioned transplanting is "cultural overhang."

> Nowhere can the "cultural overhang" more greatly damage a younger Church than in theological training. A seminary which takes its curriculum and its standards from the famous seminaries of the West is in grave danger. It forgets that to the Churches of the West great numerical increase is neither necessary for survival nor possible. . . . Hence we should discover and include in the curriculum of the younger seminaries subjects that will help students to multiply the churches they serve.[2]

The danger can be summarized by saying that in Africa, Asia, and Latin America, by and large the theological curriculum has followed the traditional Western pattern. It has not sufficiently emphasized evangelism. It has scarcely mentioned the possibility of winning groups, families, and tribes. The program has largely followed the accepted tradition of seeking intellectual and spiritual young men and women and training them away from their immediate environment. For that study the students have often received some manner of compensation. The training has been limited in its thinking to the approach used in nations where churches are firmly established. It has failed to look for great ingatherings either through individual conversions or through group or people movements.

The emphasis has often centered on *perfecting* rather than on *discipling*[3]—on building "tall towers"[4] rather than on harvesting. As a final summary on this section concerning impediments to unprecedented ingatherings, we cite McGavran again:

> What part does training play in producing men who make the churches multiply? To date it has played chiefly a negative part. Great denominations East and West—secure in hundreds of thousands of members and burdened with care of their existing churches—train their clergymen chiefly in how to shepherd the existing flocks. . . . Even those whom God lays hold of as apostles to the Gentiles are likely to leave Gamaliel's feet knowing more about how the people of God may be led farther along the pilgrim way than about how people of the world may be led to Christ.[5]

Discussion Questions

1. How do the seven factors favorable to growth in Guatemala apply to the training program with which you are presently involved? Discuss the merits of each factor, and rearrange the seven factors in their order of importance as you see it.

2. Which of the ten factors not favorable to growth in Guatemala are applicable to your situation? How important are they to the accomplishing of the objectives you have set for theological education in your own cultural environment?

1. Melvin L. Hodges, *On the Mission Field: The Indigenous Church* (Chicago: Moody, 1953), p. 58.
2. Donald A. McGavran, *How Churches Grow* (London: World Dominion, 1959), p. 142.
3. In the 1980s "discipling" is being used to refer to development in discipleship. The force of Matthew 28:19 would indicate the term means winning unbelievers to be followers of Christ. The development comes in verse 20 under "teaching them."
4. McGavran's phrase for ethical giants that represent the best in Western Christianity, built on the heritage of the past.
5. McGavran, p. 82.

5

The Nature of the Church:
The Church, Ministry, and
Theological Education

Ralph R. Covell

Theological education cannot be discussed without considering the church and its ministry. The nature of the church determines the nature of the ministry. The nature of the ministry dictates the nature and form of theological education. As we understand the nature of the church, we know whom we train, why we train them, how we train them, and what is the content of the training. Each facet of the nature of the church should tell us something about theological education.

In the Acts of the Apostles, those who make up the church are called by many different names. For example, we note that the followers of Jesus are referred to as *disciples* (6:1). They have a relationship to Christ of learning. They have come to Him and are learning from Him (Matt. 11:28-30). Those who follow Christ are also called *brethren*. They belong to the family of God

RALPH R. COVELL (Ph.D., Denver University) is professor of missions at Conservative Baptist Seminary, Denver, Colorado. For twenty years Dr. Covell was a missionary with the Conservative Baptist Foreign Mission Society in China and Taiwan. He translated the New Testament into the Sediq language of Taiwan and for five years was principal of Taiwan Baptist Theological College.

through their relationship with Jesus Christ. The *family of disciples* was first called *Christian* at Antioch (Acts 11:26). That was not a self-chosen name. The followers of Christ made it so evident that they were related to Him that they were called *Christ*ians. The disciples are also referred to as those belonging to the Way (9:2), an undoubted reference to Jesus' statement, "I am the way, and the truth, and the life" (John 14:6). Finally, those who followed Jesus are called "those who believed" (Acts 4:32). The early church, in its initial experience as recorded for us in the book of Acts, is made up of those who have made a definite personal commitment to Christ.

Even though many terms are used to refer to the followers of Jesus, the word *church* is not used extensively in Acts. It is primarily used to refer to believers in one particular locality who have come together to worship God, fellowship with one another, and serve Christ. The concept of an institutional church is often rejected today. In that view, the church is thought of as merely a spiritual organism. Idealistically, and even theologically, that may be very true, but when we look at the church in the New Testament, we see that it has a body, is very visible, and is tangible. Its locality, its nationality, its particularity are essential marks of its very being. It is not comparable to a school of Stoic or Epicurean philosophers whose existence in a given place is quite accidental.

But we do note in Acts that there are a few places where the church is referred to in terms that go beyond a merely local sense. For example, Luke recorded that "the church throughout all Judea and Galilee and Samaria enjoyed peace, being built up; and, going on in the fear of the Lord and in the comfort of the Holy Spirit, it continued to increase" (Acts 9:31). The term is used in such a way as to embrace all the people of God in those several localities. Paul reminded the elders of the Ephesian church, "Be on guard for yourselves and for all the flock, among which the Holy Spirit has made you overseers, to shepherd the church of God which He purchased with His own blood" (Acts 20:28). Because the church is described as belonging to the Lord and as having been purchased with His own blood, it refers to a group beyond one local congregation.

The church, then, in Acts is that group of people who are disciples of Christ, who are brethren in Him, who have the name Christian, who have identified themselves with the Way, Jesus Christ, and who have committed themselves as believers to Him. Every kind of person and every level of society is included within that community. There are Greek-speaking Hebrews, Hebrew-speaking Hebrews, and Greek-speaking Gentiles who, because of their past association with Jewish synagogues, are God-fearers. Also within that fellowship are Greek-speaking Gentiles who have come directly to faith in Christ from a life of superstitious idolatry.

What do we learn about theological education when we note the heterogeneity of the church and its inclusion within itself of various subcultures and many different levels of society? One apparent observation is that leaders must be trained within each group represented in the church fellowship. That will dictate a multicultural approach difficult to accomplish in our present kind of seminary program.

The church has a threefold relationship. It is a community related *vertically* to the triune God. Member relationships knit the church into a tight family fellowship internally. Finally, the church is related *outwardly* to the world, where it is to serve and proclaim the message of Christ.

THE CHURCH AND GOD

Of first importance is the relationship of the church to the triune God. *The church is a fellowship made up of those who have been called by God the Father to His salvation.* Peter enunciates clearly that "you are A CHOSEN RACE, A royal PRIESTHOOD, A HOLY NATION, A PEOPLE FOR God's OWN POSSESSION, that you may proclaim the excellencies of Him who has called you out of darkness into His marvelous light" (1 Pet. 2:9). The church is a called people. They have been taken from the bondage of sin, from the sphere of ignorance toward God, from a state of darkness, and they have been brought by God into His marvelous light.

They are aware of the fact that the condition in which they now exist is different from the one they formerly had. Much discussion is occurring today about the possibility of a person being an anonymous Christian. He is living his life for Christ and he is related to Christ, we are told, even though he may not have heard anything about Christ. That experience was not familiar to members of the New Testament church. They had a self-consciousness that they were God's own people, commissioned to declare His wonderful deeds in the world.

93

The church is a community that belongs to Jesus Christ. We note again Acts 20:28, "Be on guard for yourselves and for all the flock, among which the Holy Spirit has made you overseers, to shepherd the church of God which He purchased with His own blood." The church is a redeemed people, neither belonging to nor existing for itself. Paul unites those two aspects of the church's calling by God and its possession by Jesus Christ in 1 Thessalonians 2:14, where he refers to "the churches of God in Christ Jesus that are in Judea."

In the third place, the church is a community related to the Holy Spirit. It is a charismatic community.[1] That truth is very evident from the second chapter of Acts. Those gathered together in Jerusalem had created a great stir. Bystanders heard the wonderful works of God spoken of in their own languages. They were amazed and did not know what that meant. Peter, using the Old Testament prophecies recorded in Joel, reminded them that it was the fulfullment of God's promises. The early church was conscious of the fact that the Holy Spirit had come upon them, that He had given to them a specific work to do, and that He had equipped them with particular gifts to do that work. Theirs was the original mission impossible. And yet, being equipped supernaturally by the power of the Holy Spirit, it became mission accomplished.

Charles Dodd points out that a part of the giveness of the gospel, a very central part of the *kerygma* preached by the early church, was the fact that that was the age of fulfillment, the age of the Holy Spirit.[2] Because of His presence, the early Christians were not merely a human institution trying vainly to be do-gooders. Rather they were God's chosen community, redeemed by Jesus Christ and filled with the Holy Spirit for a world-shaking task.

The church trains men and women who have that relationship to Christ how to proclaim and live effectively the message of reconciliation. However, the task of training will be selective. It will concentrate its efforts on those people whose Spirit-given gifts clearly evidence their divine calling.

THE CHURCH AND ITS INTERNAL RELATIONSHIPS

In the second place, those who belong to that charismatic community, purchased by Jesus Christ and called by God the Father, have a very intimate relationship with each other. The church is not merely a sum of separate individuals who have made a decision for Christ. It is a corporate body, and when we are in Christ we are more than single individuals—we are members of a family with brothers and sisters in Him. Our entire lives must be lived in relationship to other members of that fellowship. That is of the very nature of the church and not peripheral to its being. Because the church is a corporate fellowship, the exhortations of the New Testament are exhortations to a social life within that community. We are to have fellowship one with another (1 John 1). We are exhorted to love one another, to submit one to another, to help one another, to exhort one another, and to confess our sins one to another.

Those commands are not easy to obey. It is far easier to live our Christian lives to ourselves without any intimate relationship to our brothers or sisters in Christ. And yet it is through that very process that Christians are socialized and brought to maturity within the family of Jesus Christ.

The family functions as a socializing agent within our society. In my own family we have three boys, all teenagers. Each has his own room. We get along wonderfully well while we are separate and when we see each other very little. But when we are together too much, tension, dissensions, and difficulties arise. However, through those problems and the consequent maturity deriving from such relationships, our boys are socialized, they learn the values of their culture, and they are prepared to live effective lives in society.

The ethics to which we are exhorted in the New Testament are not privatized but social. Note, for example, how Paul exhorted Christians at Ephesus that "with all humility and gentleness, with patience, showing forbearance to one another in love," they should be "diligent to preserve the unity of the Spirit in the bond of peace" (Eph. 4:2-3). You cannot be lowly, meek, and patient all by yourself. You cannot forbear one another in love by yourself. You cannot maintain the unity of the Spirit merely as an isolated Christian. All of those exhortations take the family life, the social life of the Christian in his relationship with other Christians, as a foundational truth.

We constantly sense a need for each other. In Romans 1, Paul explains to the church at Rome that he wishes to bring a spiritual gift to them, and then he adds, "that is, that I may be encouraged together with you while among you, each of us by the other's faith, both yours and mine" (Rom. 1:12). He was an experienced messenger of the gospel who had established many churches for Jesus Christ. He was mature in the Christian faith. Those to whom he was writing were young Christians who had not engaged in any extensive activities in the proclamation of the gospel. Despite those facts, Paul felt that not only would he be able to strengthen their faith but that their faith, as well, could encourage and strengthen him. That indicates his concept of the nature of the church as a mutual fellowship of those belonging to Jesus Christ within the community of faith. None could grow to maturity without the help of the other. If any were weak, it was the fault of all. If any were strong, that also was the result of a common effort. The church is a family, and we cannot understand what its nature is or what task God has given to it if we lose sight of its corporate nature.

What implications for theological education does the corporate nature of the church have? For one thing, it is from within the close-knit church fellowship that leaders will emerge. Even as is the case within a family in society, a certain time is needed for the members to develop to maturity. Young men who have had limited experience with the church as a fellowship and are then separated from it by a long period of preparation will not easily be able to give mature leadership. Paul exhorts us, "Do not lay hands upon anyone too hastily" (1 Tim. 5:22). In our enthusiasm to train young leaders who have not had sufficient time for mature development within the fellowship of the church, we are coming very close to violating that command.

In the second place, we do need pastors within the church who have the ability to nurture, to admonish, to rebuke, to exhort, and to lead the flock of God.

THE CHURCH AND THE WORLD

The church's third relationship is outward toward the world. The church of Jesus Christ, by its very nature, is in the world. Thus, Paul wrote to the churches at Corinth, at Philippi, at Colossae, and at Thessalonica. Not only is the church *in* the world, it is also separated *from* the world. More specifically, it is separated from the evil of the world. For that reason, the New Testament emphasizes the church as a holy community, a group of people separated to the purposes of God and collectively referred to as saints. An obvious tension exists between the concept of being *in* the world and of being separated *from* the world. Jesus Christ felt that tension in his great intercessory prayer when he prayed, "I have given them thy word; and the world has hated them, because they are not of the world, even as I am not of the world. I do not ask Thee to take them out of the world, but to keep them from the evil one. They are not of the world, even as I am not of the world'' (John 17:14-16).

The balance between the church's presence *in* the world and its separation *from* the world comes from its commission to go *into* the world. Again Jesus prays to the Father, ''As Thou didst send Me into the world, I also have sent them into the world'' (John 17:18). The church has a relationship to the triune God. It has a responsibility to all the family members within its own fellowship. And it has a mission to the world that is best epitomized by the words of Jesus Christ when He said, ''Go therefore and make disciples of all the nations, baptizing them in the name of the Father and the Son and the Holy Spirit, teaching them to observe all that I commanded you; and lo, I am with you always, even to the end of the age'' (Matt. 28:19-20). Jesus Christ sent His disciples out to proclaim the gospel, to make disciples of men and women, and then to teach them and to train them to live in the world and to serve Him within this world.

Unfortunately, it has been easy for the church to develop a ghetto complex. In trying to be separated from the world, Christians have isolated themselves from the world and have insulated themselves from all those contacts that are natural bridges for the communication of the gospel. Their lives have been centered on themselves. They have been preoccupied with developing relationships with God and mutual relationshps within the fellowship of faith, but they have forgotten the mission to the world. Nearly everything that some members of the church do is within the context of faith. Several hours a week are spent at the church sanctuary. Their children may be sent to Christian schools. The father may belong to the Christian businessmen's club. He may play on a Christian softball team or a Christian bowling team. All the relationships of the parents and of the children are with Christian people. No time or energy is left for them to consider how they might have an effective contact with people of the world in order to live within the world the message of Jesus Christ.

At that point the nature of the church is similar to the nature of Jesus Christ Himself. He is the God-man. He has two natures, the human and the divine, which can neither be separated nor be combined. Only by coming into the world in such a fashion was He able to effect the work of redemption. In like fashion, the church has a relationship to God and to the world. They cannot be separated and they cannot be combined. Only as that balance and tension is maintained is the church able effectively to perform its ministry.

What does it mean to theological education that the church is in the world? First of all, it means that leaders must be trained who are *world oriented* in their thinking rather than merely *fellowship oriented*. One person has remarked that the early church was able to turn the world upside down because they themselves had first been turned inside out. A frequent statement heard when theological education is being discussed is "All our churches have pastors. Therefore, we do not need to have a program for training more leaders." That statement reflects the church that is turned in upon itself. The basic question is, What can we do in order that we might have more churches? That demands a program of evangelism.

Take, for example, the Presbyterian Church in Taiwan. In 1954 it launched the "Double the Church" movement. At that time the Presbyterians had four hundred churches on the plains of Taiwan. Through an extensive program of evangelism, they increased those four hundred to eight hundred by 1964. That kind of emphasis on our mission in the world will demand a particular kind of leadership—a leadership that is looking toward the world and not merely inward upon its own edification and nurture. The type of leaders adequate for that kind of ministry will be mature men who themselves are thoroughly immersed in the world, who understand it, who have contacts with its people, and who are living out their lives within real situations.

A second implication follows. If we have a task within the world, it is natural to train people where they are in order that they not lose the contacts they have. James Hopewell, formerly of the Theological Education Fund, has observed that if we were to start all over in theological education, with no presuppositions of any kind, we would hardly try to train men for a ministry in the world by first separating them completely from that world.[3]

Everything that has been said about the nature of the church—that is, its relationship to the triune God, its members' mutual relationships within its fellowship, and its relationship to the world—can be summed up very well by a New Testament phrase, "the body of Christ." The body belongs to Christ, and by implication to His Father and to the Holy Spirit. The body has many members with interdependent responsibilities, and Paul speaks extensively of them in 1 Corinthians 12. The body is the means of expression outward to the world. It is the carrier of the personality of the individual. Therefore, when we use the term "the body of Christ" we are, in effect, talking about the threefold relationship that defines the nature of the church. Even where the term "body of Christ" is not used, those foundational truths about the church are assumed.

The nature of the church is closely related to the ministry of the church. At the bottom of figure 5.1 you will notice the words "Ministry to God (Worship); Ministry to the Church (Edification); Ministry to the World (Witness and Evangelism)." Those are the objects of a theological training program, because they reflect the nature of the church. The church expresses its relationship to God by worship. Because the church is a family with mutual relationships, the need exists for a ministry of edification. And because the church is in the world it has a ministry to the world, expressed in verbal witness and in loving service.

That threefold ministry is to be exercised in a general way by all the members of the church. However, God has equiped some to exercise a unique leadership role. We may say that they have a special office. They both do their specific work and train the other members of the church to fulfill their ministries. Both the general responsibility of worship, edification, and witness and the special responsibility of leading and directing in worship, edification, and witness are under the supreme authority and guidance of Jesus Christ, the Head of the church.

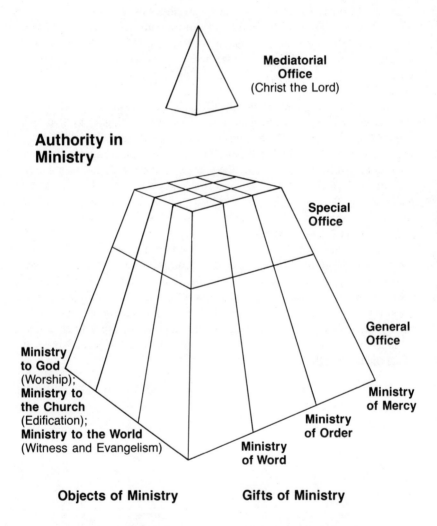

Figure 5.1. Structure of Ordered Ministry of the Church[4]

Discussion Questions

1. Discuss the threefold relationship of the church to the triune God, among its members, and to the world.
2. What implications for theological education does the corporate nature of the church have?
3. How is the nature of the church related to its threefold ministry?

1. Taken from the Greek word *charismata*. Here the word is used in its precise, biblical sense of a gifted community of believers. Each member has been gifted by the Holy Spirit with a particular ability for the corporate good and growth of the body as a whole.
2. Charles Dodd, *The Apostolic Preaching and Its Development* (New York: Harper & Row, 1936), p. 26.
3. James Hopewell, "Mission and Seminary Structure," *International Review of Missions* 56 (April 1967): 158.
4. This chart on the structure of the ordered ministry of the church was prepared by Dr. Edmund Clowney, President, Westiminster Theological Seminary, Philadelphia, Pennsylvania.

Principles of Training

6

Biblical Models for Successful Teaching

Ralph R. Covell

JESUS

The gospel records indicate that Jesus Christ was an outstanding teacher. He was called a *teacher* by His disciples, by His opponents, and by the people in general. Furthermore, all the gospels except Luke use the Aramaic *Rabbi* or its equivalent *Rabboni,* which also means "teacher."

The New Testament presents Jesus as a teacher who is both different from and similar to other teachers of that period.[1] In common with other teachers or rabbis, He had disciples. At least 90 percent of the 230 usages of the term *disciple* in the New Testament are not limited to the twelve.

Jesus was different from other rabbis in the first century in that He did not establish a formal school for the teaching of His disciples. In common with other rabbis, He had a definite content to impart, but He claimed that His teaching was directly from God. He did not depend on the authority of a particular school or upon the ordination of an important rabbi for its validity.

He taught His disciples important truths, but the crux of all His doctrine was that His disciples should be committed to Him as a person.

It is instructive to read the gospels with the precise goal of trying to understand how Jesus taught, as well as who He taught and what He taught. The concern of this section is to emphasize *how Jesus taught* and to note the potential relationship of those techniques to the concepts of TEE (theological education by extension).

1. First of all, *Jesus taught by example.*[2] Luke records that when Jesus "was praying in a certain place, after He had finished, one of His disciples said to Him, 'Lord, teach us to pray just as John also taught his disciples' " (Luke 11:1). The best kind of teaching will stimulate questions and will motivate and arouse curiosity in the learner. When Jesus taught His disciples about prayer, He did not do it with a formal lecture. He taught them how important it was to pray even when very busy. He taught them the need to pray before important decisions. He taught them that prayer is an intimate experience with God. The early church learned the intimacy and reality of prayer because of the way Jesus Himself prayed.[3]

But prayer is not the only subject Jesus taught by example. Alexander Hay has pointed out that the life of Christ provides illustrations for ten essentials for the training of disciples.[4] He sought their spiritual development. He taught them how to evangelize, to know and use the Scriptures, to have faith in God, to minister in the power of the Spirit. He led them to understand and appropriate the life and ministry of prayer in the Spirit and to be absolutely obedient to the will of God. From Him they learned to exercise unwavering faith, to love God and man, and to work together in dedication to God's will. In each of those areas it was His example, more than it was His systematized instruction, that enabled them to know what they ought to be and do.

Some have suggested that teaching by example is more difficult in theological education by extension than it is in the traditional seminary program. The argument is that the limited amount of time the teacher is able to spend with the pupil is not sufficient for the teacher to be seen as a good example. However, if the teacher utilizes the weekly relationship with his pupils to learn more about their homes, their families, and their work, possibly staying at the place of weekly meeting overnight, extension training affords a better opportunity to the teacher to be an example than would ordinarily be the case in a resident program.

2. In the second place, *Jesus Christ taught His disciples in living situations.* With Him there was no dichotomy of classroom and life. Every situation was real; there was no artificiality. Teaching was always relevant because the disciples were involved in the world. No necessity existed for Jesus periodically to make spot announcements about the need for His disciples to be relevant to the world. Jesus was teaching them on a grass-roots level. They themselves were aware of the need, because they were living in and through the situation with Christ.

When the disciples came down from the Mount of Transfiguration, they were confronted by a man with a particular problem. His son was possessed of an evil spirit who threw him into the fire and into the water. The disciples were unable to do anything for the afflicted young man. When Jesus came, He called for the father to bring his son to Him. He rebuked the evil spirit and cast him out, and the boy was cured immediately. After the man and his son had gone away, the disciples came to Jesus and asked, ''Why could we not cast it out?'' Jesus replied, ''This kind cannot come out by anything but prayer'' (Mark 9:28-29).

Suppose that Jesus had used a more traditional form of education. He might have given a lecture on the subject of evil spirits. He would have spoken first about evil spirits that can be expelled through prayer. The second point of his lecture would be that, in addition to prayer, there is frequent necessity to fast (some manuscripts add ''and fasting'' at the end of verse 29). The disciples would have taken copious notes on everything that Jesus had said about evil spirits—about the kind that could be cast out by prayer and about the kind that demanded the use of fasting. When they left that classroom situation and went into the world, they would take their notebooks with them. Sooner or later, they would meet someone possessed of an evil spirit, at which time they would need to peruse their notebooks to find the needed material. Such learning would have been very artificial.

3. In the third place, *Jesus taught His disciples by proceeding from the known to the unknown.* He started where they were. He utilized life situations around Him that would enable Him to gain their attention. For that reason, Jesus' parables have great teaching value. Think, for example, of the expres-

sion "the gospel of the Kingdom," which Jesus often used when speaking about the Kingdom of God. The phrase has within it both that which is well known and that which is relatively unknown. The Jewish people to whom He was speaking understood the Old Testament teaching about the Kingdom. The concept had been perverted by the emphases of Judaism during the interbiblical period, but first-century Hebrews still had some concept of the Kingdom. Jesus, however, spoke about "the gospel of the Kingdom." In the Greek Old Testament, the verb we translate "to evangelize" is found two or three times, but the noun "gospel" is not used. That term and its concept were new, and Jesus could put into *gospel* the content He desired. By linking the two terms *the gospel* and *the Kingdom*, he was talking at once about something the people knew and about something they did not know.

4. In the fourth place, *the teaching of Jesus was personalized.* It was individualized in accordance with the need of the person to whom Jesus was speaking. Everyone has general needs. If we are talking about the gospel of Christ, we recognize that each person is a sinner and that he needs to confess his sin, trust Christ as his personal Savior, and commit his way to Christ in a life of discipleship. People, however, not only have general needs, they also have specific needs. And the best teaching will relate itself in a particular way to the needs people individually have. Think of Jesus' conversation with the rich young ruler. Here was a young man who asked Him, "Good Teacher, what shall I do to inherit eternal life?" (Mark 10:17). Jesus reminded him of the commandments, which he had long known. When the young man heard those statements, he protested that he had obeyed all those commandments from the time he was very young. Jesus then gave to him a specific commandment, "One thing you lack: go and sell all you possess, and give to the poor, and you shall have treasure in heaven; and come, follow me" (Mark 10:21).

As far as the New Testament record goes, Jesus did not place a similar demand on any other person who came to Him. That young man had a particular need. He could not follow Christ unless he had come to grips with what was the central sin of his life. Only if he had responded to Christ in terms of that basic problem would he truly have become a disciple. Our teaching and our preaching are often so general that they never get behind the facade people have erected as a barrier between themselves and God. We need to take the time to understand the needs, problems, and difficulties people have; then we should personalize our teaching in such a way that by the power of the Holy Spirit people are brought face to face with the specific demands of Christ.

One of the difficulties in our traditional seminary program is that we lump together students of different educational and Christian backgrounds and expect to teach them all by utilizing the same methods and the same content. There is no provision, apart from counseling sessions, to make the educational process personal.

5. In the fifth place, *Jesus Christ trained by evaluating people*. That was a part of the learning process. When the seventy returned from the mission on which He had sent them, they were very happy because demons were subject to them in Christ's name. He quickly reminded them that the true cause for joy was never to be their own accomplishments, but rather what God had done for them. "Rejoice that your names are recorded in heaven" (Luke 10:20).

On another occasion, when they were sailing across the Sea of Galilee, Jesus and His disciples were involved in a tremendous storm. He noted their fear and asked, "Why are you so timid? How is that you have no faith?" (Mark 4:40). At another time, He rebuked them even more sharply because they had forgotten the lesson of the feeding of the five thousand and the feeding of the four thousand.

If we merely impart content to our students and do not take the time to know them, understand them, and live with them to the degree that we are able to evaluate them, we are not fully educating them. The traditional school does not afford us a good context in which to evaluate the total life of the student. We are able to tell how he does in his courses, how he is able to articulate, whether he does better on an objective test or on an essay test, and whether or not he turns assignments in on time. However, we often know little about many of those things that will cause him to succeed or fail in his ministry.

Theological education by extension affords a better context in which to evaluate the student. Those being trained are mature leaders already working in the church. They are educated in an environment closely related to the church. Therefore, the evaluation can easily be done by members of the churches in which the students are serving. That evaluation is much more complete, because the church is able to see the student in the total environment in which he is living.

6. Finally, *Jesus taught His disciples by delegating important work to them.* The best example of that is to be found in Matthew 28, in which Jesus is seen committing to His disciples the Great Commission. They were far from perfect at that time. In fact, Matthew records, "And when they saw Him, they worshiped Him; but some were doubtful" (Matt. 28:17). It was to those doubting, fearful, imperfect disciples of His that Jesus gave the Great Commission. He had confidence that they would be able to carry out that "mission impossible." Nothing will help a student to learn faster or to seek to implement his teaching in a better way than to know that his teacher has confidence in him. Jesus not only gave them the command, He promised them His own presence, and He promised them the direction and the power of the Holy Spirit. The task of teaching around the world often is made more difficult because we do not seem to believe that what God the Holy Spirit has done in our lives He is able also to do in the lives of those whom we teach.

Jesus Christ is the model teacher. He taught by example. He taught in living situations. He taught by proceeding from the known to the unknown. His teaching was personalized. As He taught He evaluated the lives of His students. He had confidence in them. He delegated important work to them. It was those disciples, those students who had learned under the model teacher, who took His gospel to the ends of the Roman Empire.[5]

PAUL

Teaching was central in the ministry of the apostle Paul. He considered himself a teacher (1 Tim. 2:7; 2 Tim. 1:11), and he was careful to urge that ministry upon those for whom he was responsible. Throughout the pastoral espistles we constantly see Paul's exhortation to teach (1 Tim. 4:11; 6:2; 2 Tim. 2:2). Paul clearly recognized the importance of teaching in the lives of those who were his colleagues in making Christ known.

Not only did Paul believe that he and his fellow workers had been called to teach, he also saw teaching as a responsibility of all Christians.

1. *Paul used a variety of techniques in his teaching ministry.* They can be understood by noting the terms Luke uses to describe Paul's teaching.

Paul stayed a year and six months in Corinth (Acts 18:11) "teaching [*di-*

dasko] the word of God among them.'' *Didasko* implies ''to reduce a subject to its simplest essentials, to analyze it point by point, to fix its meaning by positive and negative definition, to show how each part links with the rest—and to go on explaining'' until the hearers have grasped it.[6] It is no mere once-for-all proclamation under the assumption that once I have said it, the learner certainly has learned it. Rather, it is an explanation and a communication of truth in a variety of ways until the learner has comprehended what is involved.

So often we think that evangelism or preaching occurs prior to the point of decision and that Christian education begins only after a person has received Christ. With Paul, however, Christian education in its broadest sense was a part of his evangelistic ministry. He understood that one of the best ways, if not the best way, to preach the gospel is by teaching.

Another word used by Luke to describe Paul's teaching ministry is the verb *suzeeteo* translated ''to dispute'' (Acts 9:29—''arguing''). He not only spoke, but he also allowed his listeners to speak and to ask questions. He sought to understand their point of view at the same time that he was presenting his perspective.

A third word used frequently by Luke is *dialego* (''dialogue,'' or ''reason''): Paul ''was reasoning in the synagogue every Sabbath'' (Acts 18:4); ''reasoning . . . about the kingdom of God'' (Acts 19:8). That was not a monologue, a lecture, or one-way communication. Paul was ready to allow his hearers to give him feedback that then enabled him to clarify the truth he was presenting. That two-way communication process did not mean that Paul was deficient in his convictions, because along with the verbs ''argue'' and ''reason,'' Luke records that Paul ''persuaded'' Jews and Greeks about the Kingdom of God (Acts 18:4; 19:8). Paul did not teach truth abstractly. He would not have fallen into the error of those who frequently say, ''It is my responsibility to teach and God will give the results.'' Paul knew that he himself had an obligation to persuade. He had a burden not only to make Christ known but, by the power of the Holy Spirit, to seek to lead men to a commitment to Christ. His was not a disinterested communication. He pled with men to be reconciled to God (2 Cor. 5:20).

2. *Paul had a definite content to be taught.* A second thing to be noted

about Paul's principles of teaching is that he believed he had a definite message to be communicated.

He frequently used words that mean "tradition," either in verbal or noun forms ("delivered"—1 Cor. 15:3; "entrust"—2 Tim. 2:2). That tradition had a definite *doctrinal* content. In the 1 Corinthians 15:3-4 formulation it included the death, burial, and resurrection of Jesus Christ. The apostolic tradition also provided *ethical exhortation* for the early church.[7] Paul commanded Christians at Thessalonica to "keep aloof from every brother who leads an unruly life and not according to the tradition which you received from us" (2 Thess. 3:6).

The source of the doctrinal or ethical tradition used by Paul was at least threefold:

a) First of all was the Old Testament. Early believers apparently had available to them an informal oral or written tradition of Old Testament quotations commonly used by the church.

b) Paul also made extensive use of the words of Jesus. He seldom quoted Jesus verbatim, but he frequently alluded to His words. One German scholar has noted nearly one thousand allusions to the words of Jesus in the teaching of Paul.[8]

c) A third source of the tradition that Paul had received was the informal or even more formal teaching materials used by the early church.

Whether the Old Testament, the words of Jesus, or those early teaching materials, Paul was clear that the ultimate source of that which he had received and for which he was responsible was God Himself.[9]

Despite the fact that Paul knew he was passing on a definite content, two factors guided his presentation:

a) In the first place, *Paul was clear that his goal was not merely to impart knowledge but to teach obedience.* The end point of his teaching process was not to evaluate how much the learner was able to memorize or to repeat back to him. The basic question was, Is this truth lived out now in your life in obedience?

In his relationship with the Corinthian church, Paul reminded the people there that he was sending Timothy, "my beloved and faithful child in the Lord, and he will remind you of my ways which are in Christ, just as I teach everywhere in every church" (1 Cor. 4:17). He then went on to point out that "my ways which are in Christ" were to be obeyed, because "the kingdom of God does not consist in words, but in power" (1 Cor. 4:20).

The same emphasis on obedience is seen in the Great Commission, in which Jesus commanded His disciples to "go therefore and make disciples of all the nations, . . . teaching them to *observe* all that I commanded you" (Matt. 28:19-20, italics added). The aim of their teaching was not to impart knowledge but to produce obedient disciples.

In my contact with the Taroko tribe in Taiwan, I have often been impressed with how little they know but how well they obey what they know. At the beginning of their movement toward Christ they really knew only three truths. They were sure that God loved them and that He had sent His Son to die for their sins. In the second place, they knew that a Christian must suffer persecution when he believed. Third, they knew the power and the priority of prayer. From our sophisticated viewpoint those may not appear to be profound truths. However, because of their thorough obedience God poured out such a blessing upon the mountain peoples of Taiwan that one out of every three believed in Christ in a movement that has been called the "Pentecost of the Hills."

b) Paul also changed the form of his message to suit the differing audiences to which he was speaking. In Acts 13, Paul speaks to a congregation of Jewish people. In the following chapter Luke describes his approach to a group of very superstitious and idolatrous Gentiles. On Mars Hill (Acts 17) Paul is again speaking to men immersed in idolatry and superstition, but they are intellectual leaders in the city of Athens. In each instance the gospel content assumes a different shape. The central core of the message is the same, but Paul does not communicate it to the people in the same way.

We have been very negligent in this matter. Uncritically, we have said that the gospel is the same for all people. By that we correctly mean that all men are alienated from God, that they need a Savior, and they are saved by putting their trust in Jesus Christ, the crucified, buried, resurrected, and ascended Savior. Those are eternal truths, but the ways in which we present them, those things which we are going to emphasize, and the ways in which we will relate those truths to what the people already know, are going to be different in each situation. If we neglect the fact that our hearer is different in differing situations, we will not communicate the gospel in the way Paul did.

3. *Paul was selective in his training process.* He exhorted Timothy, "The things which you have heard from me in the presence of many witnesses, these entrust to faithful men, who will be able to teach others also" (2 Tim. 2:2). Paul had a team of men who worked with him. Those men were gifted, not necessarily because of natural talents, but because they had received gifts of the Holy Spirit that enabled them to teach. Their call had been verified by their gifts.

They were faithful from the negative standpoint because they loyally guarded the tradition that they had received. Positively, they were committed to passing on that tradition. It would not stop them. They were able to teach others because of their gifts, and they were ready to teach others because they were committed, faithful men.

A common problem in all of our training schools is that we have very young people coming to us who, when they are questioned as to their reasons for wanting to study, will usually say, "I have been called to serve God." We are not as careful as we ought to be to seek concrete evidence that they have gifts that would prepare them for the ministry and that would validate their calling.

Paul taught his team in a variety of ways. They traveled with him and saw the way in which he worked. He gave them responsibilities to fulfill. He delegated them to go and visit churches where they had previously worked together as a team. Paul carried books with him, and, undoubtedly, used some of those books as a means of teaching his team. His ways in Christ were known to them (1 Cor. 4:17), and that apprenticeship training prepared them to fulfill the ministry that God had given them in the churches.

4. *Paul made Christ the center of the content taught in the churches.* He exhorted the Christians at Ephesus, "But you did not learn Christ in this way, if indeed you have heard Him and have been taught in Him just as truth is in Jesus that, in reference to your former manner of life, you lay aside the old

self, which is being corrupted in accordance with the lusts of deceit, and that you be renewed in the spirit of your mind, and put on the new self, which in the likeness of God has been created in righteousness and holiness of the truth'' (Eph. 4:20-24). Christ was the content and goal of the teaching, and, in reality, Christ Himself, by the Holy Spirit, was teaching through Paul. The end product of Paul's teaching was that the learner might be like Jesus Christ.

Here is a solid foundation for an indigenous theology. We are not merely teaching a factual content, much of which may have accretions developed within our North American culture. We are not merely teaching Christ as He has been understood by our sending churches. We are not merely going through a stereotyped process of using human methodology, techniques, and resources to teach. Rather, we are presenting the Christ of God's unique revelation. He is freed from the specific cultural baggage that has developed about His person in our society. He will become incarnate, as it were, in the target culture. In that way, we will have what we can call Indian Christians, African Christians, and Chinese Christians. Those believers will not necessarily think alike, feel alike, or act alike. They will have their own personal relationship to Jesus Christ, which will express itself uniquely in the culture where they are.

That does not mean that their faith will not have common elements with the faith of Christians in other countries. Yes, it certainly will have. A Christian is a Christian because of his relationship to the Christ presented in God's Word. That, however, is far different from saying that a Chinese Christian must think and feel and act the same way an American Christian does.

The world is filled with an abundance of excellent ethical systems. If we who teach the Christian faith do not make it very clear that the uniqueness of Christianity is in the person of Jesus Christ Himself, the world will wrongly read us to understand that the Christian message is only one more system of morality.

5. *Paul taught principles, not specific details.* The best example of that is the first Corinthian epistle. That church had many problems, and the believers came to Paul to seek solutions. He answered by enunciating principles that could answer the current problems and give guidelines for solving future difficulties. Paul had great confidence in the Holy Spirit, who would interpret the principles of the Christian life in the believers' experiences.

Roland Allen is well known for his book *Missionary Methods: St. Paul's or Ours?* (New York: Samuel R. Leland, 1913). Another book written by him that has not been so widely acclaimed is *The Spontaneous Expansion of the Church* (Grand Rapids: Eerdmans, 1962). Here Allen argues persuasively that Paul did not hedge his churches about with minute details and regulations to predetermine everything they should do. He committed the principles of God's Word to them, encouraged them to trust the Holy Spirit, and taught them to develop their own lives in an indigenous manner fitting to the environment in which they were living. The result of that approach? Instant indigenous church.[10]

Our task, therefore, in teaching is to give people the principles of God's Word and some examples on how to apply those principles in concrete, life situations. Furthermore, we must reserve immediate judgment on questionable issues, allow the Holy Spirit freedom to direct, and believe that God is able to work in their lives even as He works in ours.

Paul was not stereotyped in his teaching. He used a variety of techniques. Although he recognized that there was a definite content to be taught, he did not present facts as an end in themselves but as a means to lead the learner to obedience. Moreover, he communicated that content differently for each audience to whom he was speaking. And, Paul did not believe that everyone could be a teacher on the church-leadership level. Therefore, he evaluated carefully who had gifts of the Holy Spirit for teaching, and concentrated his efforts on them. His teaching centered on Jesus Christ. He taught people to discover the principles of God's Word, and then he helped them as they tried to apply those truths to living situations.[11]

Discussion Questions

1. How do the six techniques used by Jesus in His teaching relate to the concepts of theological education by extension? Discuss each one and its potential value in the program of education in your church or school.
2. In what ways was Jesus' teaching similar to that of other teachers of His day? In what respect did it differ from theirs and to what degree?
3. What five things made Paul successful in his teaching? Were his methods flexible? In what ways? Compare his methods with those of Jesus.

1. Much of this material is from Karl H. Rengstorf, "Didasko," *Theological Dictionary of the New Testament,* ed. Gerhard Kittel, English ed. (Grand Rapids: Eerdmans, 1964), 2:138-43.
2. I am indebted to Dr. Howard Hendricks of Dallas Theological Seminary for the general outline of this chapter.
3. Joachim Jeremias, *The Prayers of Jesus* (Naperville, Ill.: Allenson, 1967), pp. 11-65.
4. Alexander Hay, *The New Testament Order for Church and Missionary* (Buenos Aires, Argentina: New Testament Missionary Union, 1947), supplement to chapter 4.
5. Books of value on Jesus as a teacher are: A. B. Bruce, *The Training of the Twelve* (Edinburgh: T. & T. Clark, 1908); Robert E. Coleman, *The Master Plan of Evangelism* (New York: Revell, 1964); H. H. Horne, *Jesus the Master Teacher* (Grand Rapids: Kregel, 1968).
6. J. I. Packer, *Evangelism and the Sovereignty of God* (Chicago: InterVarsity, 1961), p. 48.
7. Ian Muirhead, *Education in the New Testament* (New York: Association Press, 1965), pp. 49-64.
8. Otto Roller, *Das Formular Der Paulinischen Briefe* (Stuttgart: W. Kohlhammer, 1933).
9. For a concise treatment of the source of Paul's tradition see Archibald Hunter, *Paul and His Predecessors,* rev. ed. (Philadelphia: Westminster, 1961).
10. Allen also develops this thesis in chapter 4, "St. Paul and the Judaizers: A Dialogue," of his book *The Ministry of the Spirit* (Grand Rapids: Eerdmans, 1962).
11. A classic book helpful in any consideration of Paul as a teacher is Howard T. Kuist, *The Pedagogy of Paul* (n.p.: Doran, 1925).

7

A Practical Approach: Theological Education in Honduras

George Patterson

AN EDUCATIONAL PHILOSOPHY GROWING OUT OF PERSONAL EXPERIENCE

Obedience-oriented education, as developed in Honduras, grew out of a TEEE program, which grew out of a TEE program, which grew out of a TE program. Let me explain:

TE stands for theological education. It is usually related to a resident seminary or Bible institute.

GEORGE PATTERSON (Th. M., D.D., Western Conservative Baptist Seminary) serves as a missionary under the Conservative Baptist Home Mission Society and has been engaged in church planting in Honduras since 1965.

TEE stands for theological education by extension. It takes pastoral studies to the student, where he is. It reaches men who cannot leave their homes or jobs. It relates their studies to their local-church work in the community, and it does not take place in the seclusion of a resident seminary. Self-teaching textbooks permit less time spent in the classroom, but they require more private study. Unfortunately, TEE often results merely in education rather than in evangelization or in the starting of new churches.

TEEE integrates evangelism with TEE. It aims primarily at *building churches* in the New Testament sense. It defines the goal of evangelism not as "soul-winning" but as the birth and growth of churches.

How did the Honduras Extension Bible Institute come to apply TEEE? Our TEEE program proved to be an efficient tool for planting new churches and evangelizing the lost. TEEE strengthened rather than weakened the school's educational capacity by broadening its scope. That happy joining of education and evangelism blossomed only as we oriented the education toward obedience. Workers and churches multiplied in a way unknown to the former TE program.

Obedience orientation is not just a method. It is a way of thinking and acting in obedience to Christ. It is applicable to the resident seminary, the extension institute, or the local church whose pastor trains a "Timothy" in order to multiply his own ministry. If we start with absolute obedience to Christ, disregarding tradition, we arrive at the following requirements for theological education:

1. IT MUST BE DIRECTLY RELATED TO A LOCAL CHURCH

In Honduras, the heart of our pastoral course is our love for the Lord Jesus Christ. Obedience for any other motive is legalism. He said, "If you love Me, you will keep My commandments" (John 14:15). That love is cultivated through the local church. The student does not work for the professor, for grades, or for a diploma; he works because of his love for edifying the Body of Christ.

Christ gave the authority to educate His people to the church—not to an autonomous seminary (Matt. 28:18-20). The seminary working within that sphere of authority finds the local church to be its most valuable classroom. A seminary remaining independent of the churches can hardly have an obedience-oriented curriculum. The theological institution should place itself neither over nor under the local church, but in a cooperative with it. At the same time, each local church must incubate pastors in collaboration with the resident or extension seminary.

A biblical principle of Christian education demands: ''Prove yourselves doers of the word, and not merely hearers who delude themselves'' (James 1:22). The apostle apparently denounces any educational process that results in passive learning. Many traditional pastoral courses do just that. The student, conditioned by three or four years of passively learning the Word, graduates with an institutional mentality. He treats his church as if it were a small Bible institute. The people sit and learn passively. The church, instead of being the sensitive, creative body God intended it to be, becomes pastor-centered and passive.

In Honduras, all practical work assignments are done in direct obedience to Christ. We do not simply hand out Christian service assignments over the weekend or assign each student to a church. The practical work is an integral part of the pastoral course. We develop it by starting with the commands of Christ for His churches. We determine the necessary steps for carrying out His Great Commission in our area of responsibility. His orders form the backbone of our curriculum. The congregational activities necessary to carry them out make up the skeleton of the course.

The flesh appears on our pastoral training course as we state those activities in terms of specific places, people, and responsibilities. Our general objective may be to train men to start new churches; our immediate objective is to train Jim Brown to start a new church on Seventh Street this year. Our general objective may be to prepare men to witness; our immediate objective is for student-worker Carl Smith to mobilize laymen Sanchez, Johnson, and Woods to witness this weekend. An obedience-oriented education requires immediate objectives with names, places, and dates.

In a new church, the student may win the first converts and work with them to bring them to maturity. He learns and grows along with his congregation. In an established church the student wins converts and brings them to maturity as a group within the larger congregation.

We have an obedience-initiated pastoral course when our immediate educational objectives fulfill the commands of Christ. To guarantee a permanent orientation to obedience we must secure the active cooperation and participation of the members of already existing local churches. It is hard to change a very traditional church as a body, but there are usually members who are eager to cooperate, without pushing those who lack enthusiasm.

2. ITS CURRICULUM MUST FIT THE LOCAL SITUATION

Ephesians 1:17-23 gives us insight into the divine process of theological education: God Himself gives His people (the members of the local church in Ephesus) a spirit of wisdom and revelation to know Him and His program. The teacher must help his student-worker to participate in that divine educational process. What he studies should correspond to the activities of the local church where he works. Essential elements of doctrine, Bible, and church history are introduced into his course where they best meet the needs of those people for whom he is responsible. We do not give doctrine and Bible a lower place in the obedience-oriented curriculum: they take on a surprisingly new importance when related directly to the life and activities of a growing congregation. That requires constant communication between the teacher and the churches—the nervous system of the pastoral course. (See figure 7.1.)

The two-way communication between teacher and student-worker is as vital as that between a military commander and his trainees. During a long campaign the troops are repeatedly briefed and oriented. After they have obtained one objective and are getting ready for their next encounter, they are reequipped with rubber rafts, snowshoes, gas masks, or antitank weapons, according to the intelligence reports and the commander's directive. The pastoral student may not need to learn how to inflate a rubber raft, but he will need to know how to discipline a disorderly member of a new congregation. For that he needs special equipment. His teacher must know what his work is and relate the theoretical studies to it.

PARTICIPATION WITH THE CHURCHES IN THE DIVINE EDUCATIONAL PROCESS

• • •

A traditional view of the educational process:

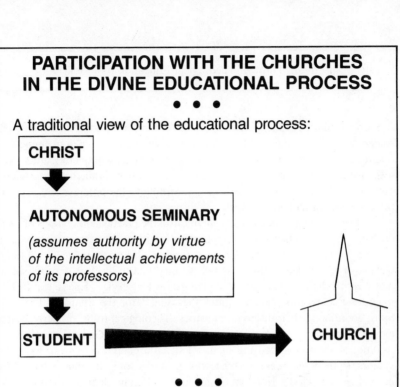

• • •

Two-way communication in the educational process:

Picture the student walking back and forth from the church to the teacher. From the church he takes progress reports, needs, and information about the field. From the teacher, primed by these reports, he carries solutions, materials, and instruction for the church's progress.

Figure 7.1

Such teaching is challenging; it spoils us for the conventional classroom. The student-worker also devours his studies with an eagerness seldom found in a traditional institution. He is obeying Christ! As part of a conquering army, he is responsible for his part of the work in the local church. Immediate educational objectives change from week to week, according to the progress and needs of those for whom the student-worker is responsible.

The teacher must enable his student to fulfill the practical obligations of every doctrine. We do not tack on an "application" to it: rather, we approach doctrine out of a primary desire to obey Christ. A teacher who cannot relate his subject to the life of his student's church is not yet qualified to teach it. Pastors should mobilize all the members of the congregation for service. Ephesians 4:11-16 indicates that pastors should equip "the saints" for the ministry. The Holy Spirit coordinates their different ministries. Theological truth, properly taught, moves us to serve together as a body. The Spirit of God relates different theological truths by focusing them on specific church activities. Too often systematic theology seeks to relate divine truths logically, but outside their normal setting. God's Holy Spirit integrates different elements of Bible doctrine, history, Christian education, and so forth as they apply to men's lives, struggles with the world, contradicting philosophies, politics, and human relationships. (See figure 7.2.)

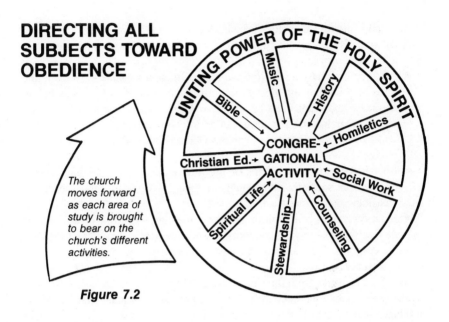

DIRECTING ALL SUBJECTS TOWARD OBEDIENCE

The church moves forward as each area of study is brought to bear on the church's different activities.

Figure 7.2

The teacher of the obedience-oriented pastoral course is responsible for his student's weekly progress. He teaches the same general content as the traditional seminary or Bible institute professor, but not in the same order. He gives his student what he needs for his own changing needs as he takes on more and more responsibility in his church.

3. ITS PROGRAM MUST PERMIT SPONTANEOUS DEVELOPMENT OF THE CHURCH

Mark 4:26-29 illustrates how churches take root, grow, and develop their different ministries spontaneously, with a minimum of control on the part of the workers responsible.

We recognize the Lord Jesus Christ's supreme authority over all churches and theological institutions. Where He reigns, the church develops spontaneously. Under His sole command, the church grows and multiplies in a manner natural to herself. A normal, healthy congregation must grow and multiply. That is her very nature, built into her by the Almighty Creator.

We find in living things four principles common to created life:
- All organisms, even the simplest plants, have the capacity to reproduce after their own kind.
- All organisms have a sensitivity to react to their environment. (Even in the viruses, a kind of intelligence discerns what foreign particles can be assimilated and what must be repulsed. More complex animals learn and reason. Man has the dangerous ability to choose between right and wrong and the blessed capacity to worship God and appreciate His divine attributes.)
- All but the most basic forms of life differentiate their cells into diverse organs; that specialization enables the plant, animal, or person to do increasingly complicated activities.
- Most organisms bear fruit or provide something useful for others besides themselves; plants yield antibiotics, wood, berries, flowers, and feed for the cow, which produces milk, meat, and leather; men produce good and evil works.

The Creator works from the simple toward the more complex and useful. He began with plants, then animals; but He did not end with man. Man is not the ultimate creation; the church is. The Lord Jesus Christ arose on the first day of the week as the Head of an entirely new creation (1 Cor. 15:20-23, 40-49). That is his Body, the church.

Like all living creatures, the church has within herself the power to grow and multiply after her own kind (Mark 4:1-20). She develops spontaneously, not like an institution whose progress depends on the initiative of her executives. An active, feeling body, she seethes with potential energy. An obedient church has to grow and multiply just as surely as the plants and animals; it is her nature. That assurance moves us to witness and serve in relaxed, voluntary obedience to Christ.

The church likewise has an intelligence of her own, a spiritual nervous system: Christ the Head communicates through the Holy Spirit to each member. The church, in cooperation with qualified teachers and institutions, educates herself theologically. She discerns what doctrine she should take in or refuse. She selects and trains her own leaders. The professional educator must gear into that divine educational process. He cannot create it; nor should he seek to control it, or he kills its spontaneity. He must first of all help build relationships of love between persons—relationships that begin with Christ and flow through His church to the world about her.

Like other living creatures, the church has the power within herself to differentiate her "cells." Each member of a local church has a gift, or specialization, for ministering to the needs of the congregation. Those gifts provide for ministries that must contribute to the upbuilding of the whole body (Rom. 12:4-8; 1 Cor. 12). An active, obedient church soon discovers those different ministries that God has distributed among her members. She does not try to manufacture the pastoral gift in a classroom. An active congregation, given the liberty to do so, readily develops the necessary gifts among her members.

Like other living things, the church also produces fruit. She alone has the privilege of bearing fruit of eternal value and duration. It results, inevitably, from any work done in faith and loving obedience to the commands of Christ (John 15:1-10; 1 Cor. 3:11-15). That fruit oftens grows high on the tree; we may fail to see it from earth. It may bear little relation to the amount of effort or money invested.

Spontaneous growth is neither rare nor special. It is the normal, daily development and reproduction of any reasonably obedient congregation planted in good soil. It happens as sure as any other harvest: a normal church produces more kernels of spiritual grain (witnessing, serving, visiting, giving, etc.) than were originally sown (Mark 4:1-20). A church can produce double, triple, or a hundredfold. But if a church consumes 100 kernels per week to maintain her own program and produces an average of only 50 among her members, she requires another 50 to survive, provided by an outside worker, missionary, or mother church. Such a "sponge" only absorbs spiritual energy and impedes spontaneous growth. New churches are not automatically sponges; they often produce more spiritual energy per member than older churches.

In Honduras we observed two kinds of curriculum in a controlled "laboratory" situation. Isolated from most outside influences, village churches were almost entirely dependent for their religious education upon the efforts of our mission. We could control the theological input. We observed churches whose only input came through an obedience-oriented course. Other churches' input came through the traditional, doctrinally-oriented course. Some churches received a combination of both influences. The obedience-oriented churches grew, multiplied, maintained discipline, and showed discernment in doctrine.

The churches with the traditional, doctrinally-oriented education grew not at all except through the efforts of outside workers. Although they knew more doctrine as such, they suffered more from doctrinal error and lacked initiative. Churches influenced by both orientations did well only when they gave priority to obedience.

For education to contribute to the spontaneous multiplication of churches, the factor of self-multiplication must be part of the curriculum. That is simple. Any pastor can train a ''Timothy'' with the help of a cooperative theological institution. That Timothy, in turn, quickly begins to train his own Timothy (2 Tim. 2:2). Self-multiplication requires that every student-worker also become a student-teacher. The process can result in the multiplication of churches in remote areas where travel is difficult and people lack normal educational opportunities.

An obedience-oriented program of education deals with the changing activities of a living, growing, obedient body. Once a theological institution commits itself to release that spontaneous growth and development of Christ's church through education, its objectives, philosophy, and teaching methods will automatically improve. We measure that improvement not by the academic criteria of accrediting boards or theological associations, but by pastoral standards that seek, above all, the edification of churches. The seminary concerned with both scholarship and the Great Commission should offer two very separate courses: one for professional scholars (every denomination needs them) and another for pastors.

4. ITS EDUCATIONAL PROCESS MUST BE BY THE EXTENSION PRINCIPLE

The wise pastor multiplies his ministry in others: he prepares Timothies, who imitate him (1 Cor. 11:1; Phil. 3:17; etc.). Every pastoral student needs to observe and imitate a good pastor. In some churches everything revolves around a poor pastor. Others cannot imitate him because he gives them no responsibility in the work. They listen to him passively, occasionally doing what he says. The educational process ends with his teaching. (See figure 7.3.)

In 2 Timothy 2:2 we find four links in the chain of extension:

And the things which you have heard from me [Paul]

in the presence of many witnesses, these entrust [Timothy]

to faithful men,

who will be able to teach others also.

A PASSIVE, PASTOR-CENTERED CHURCH:

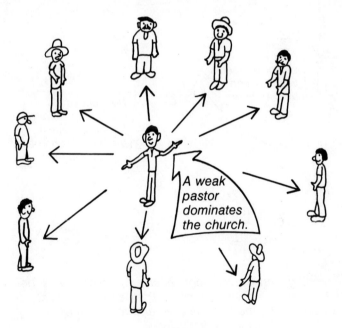

A weak pastor dominates the church.

Figure 7.3

To permit a spontaneous movement in the churches, the theological curriculum itself forms part of the multiplying process. The students become teachers of others: their assignments aim to develop new leaders in an atmosphere of freedom to work for Christ. Every man in a church should learn to take part in the ministry in some way; our students must be trained to train them. (See figure 7.4.)

INTERACTION IN A DYNAMIC CHURCH:

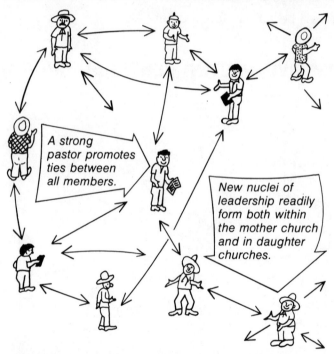

A strong pastor promotes ties between all members.

New nuclei of leadership readily form both within the mother church and in daughter churches.

Teaching and serving one another provides links between many active members. They share the pastoral responsibility; the body is alive and reproductive.

Figure 7.4

To mobilize new leadership by the extension principle of 2 Timothy 2:2 requires small, tightly disciplined classes taught by student-workers. (See figure 7.5.)

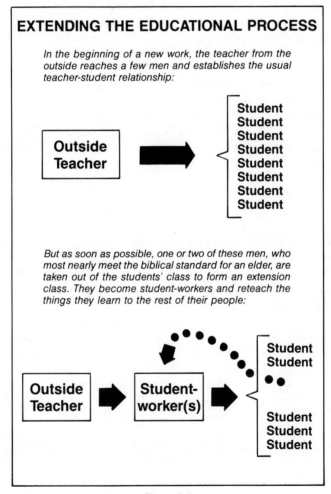

EXTENDING THE EDUCATIONAL PROCESS

In the beginning of a new work, the teacher from the outside reaches a few men and establishes the usual teacher-student relationship:

Outside Teacher → Student Student Student Student Student Student Student Student

But as soon as possible, one or two of these men, who most nearly meet the biblical standard for an elder, are taken out of the students' class to form an extension class. They become student-workers and reteach the things they learn to the rest of their people:

Outside Teacher → **Student-worker(s)** → Student Student Student Student Student

Figure 7.5

The extension class should be limited to one, two, or three men. If others want to study, one of the student-workers should teach them in another class. The use of the student-worker to teach the others has five advantages:

1. The new student-worker becomes a responsible leader.

2. The outside teacher does not weaken the local leaders when he works through them; an extension program weakens the local ministry if it takes over pastoral responsibility with the people, bypassing the local leaders for a larger class.

3. The outside teacher conserves his time. His students take most of the responsibility for their own churches, and he can deal with several churches in the same time that he would otherwise spend with one.

4. The class can deal with details of the work that could not be discussed in a large, unrestricted group which, because of its size, becomes simply another Sunday school class.

5. The educational structure is already set up for reproduction. Nothing needs to be changed for a daughter church or a new nucleus of leaders within the same church to be started. The student-worker simply repeats the same steps in another area.

Pastors and teachers who tend to be dictators impede that free extension of the educational process. They do not delegate responsibility or recognize their own students as colleagues in the educational process. They enjoy teaching but fail to trust their students to reteach the same things to others. We do not enjoy it when others impede the practice of our own spiritual gift. The ordained pastor should accept the biblical authority of the lay ministers or elders and encourage their participation (Titus 1:5). A pastor's own biblical authority lies in that he is an elder, with a special gift (Eph. 4:11-12; 1 Pet. 5:1-4). The experienced pastor should encourage, train, and trust his Timothies.

In order for a Timothy to imitate his "Paul," as an apprentice, the latter must use only equipment and methods that are within the student's reach. Everything the teacher does is to be imitated. Christ never ordered his disciples to do anything they had not observed Him doing.

Paul the apostle left new churches organized under new elders (Acts 14:23). Following his example, a church planter enters an unevangelized community, wins several men to Christ, and, after their baptism, enrolls them in an extension class to let them raise up their own church. New churches result from an education program rather than an evangelistic crusade. Such churches are stronger from the beginning and more evangelistic: their local laymen have taken the responsibility. In the resulting multiplication of daughter and grand-daughter churches, the link in the chain of spiritual reproduction is not the individual witness but the local church.

5. IT MUST BUILD INTO ITS PROGRAM A WORKABLE SYSTEM OF ACCOUNTABILITY

The theological institution, resident or extension, formal or informal, must deal regularly with the student's practical work. The pastoral student must continually orient himself in sessions that deal with his reports and plans. His teacher supervises his activities and enables him to apply everything he learns. Everything taught should contribute to the student's present ministry. No professor is teaching well unless his student is enjoying a fruitful ministry. The practical-work class[1] does not train the man for the future; it relates his training to a present pastoral experience.

An effective practical-work class will begin with each student's detailed report of his work. That limits the class to a few students; one is ideal. If many others wish to study, they may do so in separate classes, each taught by one of the regular students. Only mature men should be enrolled in a serious pastoral-work class because of the nature of their work (1 Tim. 3:1-7). In that class the teacher gives each student studies and counsel to meet the needs expressed in the student's report. In a resident seminary those studies may be arranged with the professor of the subject involved. The teacher of the practical-work class should file the needs reported from the field. Those records should be used in the preparation of textbooks and for the anticipation of problems.

In a resident institution every professor should keep in touch with the needs of the churches of the student-workers and relate his classroom studies to them. But many professors lack the qualifications for the practical-work class: only experienced pastors should attempt it. Perhaps only a few men will qualify. Time may not allow those few professors to hold many small practical-work classes. The students, however, can form teams, each with a captain in his final year. The professor has only those captains in the practical-work class; they in turn hold classes for their teams. Cooperating pastors can also hold the practical-work classes in their churches. Those pastors should have a checklist for each student's required activities.

Both extension and resident theological institutions must verify each student's progress in his practical activities. A checklist or register of his progress should depict each activity that he must do to raise up a church, edify its members, and deal with the problems that every pastor faces. That register is not simply a list of pastoral skills; it is a guide for helping a congregation to grow. The aim is to edify the church. The register, or checklist, presents a projected history of a church as it grows from infancy to maturity. It mentions congregational activities: duties of parents, deacons, Bible teachers; services for special occasions; congregational visitation; missionary projects; and community development. The new student-worker, not yet a pastor, wins a group of people to Christ and leads them through all those activities into maturity. He starts with personal witnessing and takes on more and more responsibility until at graduation he is, in fact, a pastor. The student who begins a new church and brings it to spiritual maturity (or does the same for a group within an older church) deserves his diploma. He has dealt with those needs that truly test the theory of his pastoral course: he has related his studies to a living situation.

The Honduras Extension Bible Institute offers only practical-work classes. Student-workers do almost all their own theoretical studies during their own time. Each student keeps a register of progress for each congregation with which he is working. It lists thirty-five activities, each of which requires several weekly studies. Each weekly study combines theory with a practical assignment in one small textbooklet, which is pocket-size so that it can be carried and read during the week. There are no long-term courses in Bible, history, or doctrine. The units for each activity combine relevant elements from those different areas. Some units are strictly biblical studies; others combine elements of history, theology, and homiletics all in one brief study. Some weekly-study booklets treat definite congregational needs that may arise any time. Over the years, the same needs reoccur. Although every congregation's career differs, a general pattern emerges that enables us to foresee most of the needs in the register of progress.

The teacher of the practical-work class shares the responsibility for the effective weekly ministry of his student. If his student fails, he fails; if his student succeeds, he succeeds. The proof of effective teaching is in the spontaneous growth and development of the student's congregation. The student's progress is measured primarily by the results of those activities for which the church has made him responsible.

Discussion Questions

1. Define the distinction made in Honduras between TE, TEE, and TEEE.
2. Discuss each of the five requirements for theological education in Honduras. Which, if any, of those requirements is lacking in your educational program? How can their integration into the existing structures be implemented?
3. How can a student's progress be effectively measured?

1. By a "practical-work class" we mean a session in which theory and practice are related in word and deed: subject matter taught contributes to practical assignments. Ideally, every class should be a practical-work class.

8

FOR MINISTERS ONLY:
Training *for* and *in* Ministry

Fred Holland

The proper end of theological education is *ministry*. All theological education must be part and parcel of the church and of mission. It can only be those things as it trains the ministry of the church *for* service that directly relates to the will and purpose of God. God wants us to make disciples and to bring them into worshiping and serving congregations. Training *in* service is to prepare adequate leadership so that continuing growth takes place in outreach, maturity, and organization.

One major contribution of TEE (theological education by extension) has been that we as theological educators have been forced to think seriously about ministry. What is it? What does it do? How do we train for it?

WHAT IS MINISTRY?

The Greek word *diakonia* can be translated either as "service" or as

FRED HOLLAND (D. Missiology, Fuller School of World Mission) is director of extension, Wheaton Graduate School, Wheaton, Illinois. Formerly a missionary in Rhodesia and Zambia, Dr. Holland has served as executive secretary of the Association of Evangelical Bible Institutes and Colleges of Africa and Madagascar.

"ministry." It may be thought of as function or as institution, and that gives rise to much of the debate about who performs the ministry (service) and who the ministry is.

It was the Roman Catholic writer Hans Küng who disturbed the theologians' thinking on ecclesiology and ministry when in his book *Why Priests? A Proposal for a New Church Ministry* he called for a rediscovery and use of the *total* membership for ministry. "The Church's ministry of leadership," he said, "is meant essentially not to be an autocratic authority absorbing all other functions, but one ministry in the midst of a multiplicity of . . . functions."[1]

Although such writers as Küng and Rahner add their voices to the arguments in favor of change in the laity in particular and the church in general, it will obviously be slow going. It will take new forms to implement the new functions, for if the laity are to perform ministry, they must do so equipped and encouraged by leaders.

From the early church of the book of Acts we can infer that:

1. Ministry in general is always the total service of the total Christian community, whether in relation to its own members or to others.

2. In any kind of ministry, leadership is always needed.

3. Leadership should be according to competence. And competence is ultimately functional—that is, leaders should have the combination of abilities that can best get the job done.

4. Whereas ministry focuses on communities and there outreach, special respect is to be accorded the ministry that forms lines of communication among local groups.[2]

In light of those statements, we can insist that "the seminary must serve a double purpose: the transmission of learning *and* the preparation of persons for the practice of a profession. Since it must do both, the question becomes one of proportion. Or, at a deeper level, which one governs the other? Does the information in the traditional curriculum determine the kind of ministry to be performed, or should the practice, in part at least, dictate what information should be supplied?"[3]

John V. Taylor, who is general secretary of the Church Missionary Society and is involved in theological training, says: "Our training curricula are largely a hangover from the past and are not, in the main, functionally related to the tasks for which men are being trained. And this tremendous weakness stems, in turn, from the fact that we are still unwilling to define the ministry of the Church in functional terms at all. Instead we define it still in terms of structure and authority."[4]

It will help us, therefore, to think of ministry not so much as office or position but as function. Only as we know more about what is to be done by the ministry—the function—can we adequately train people to perform that function. The New Testament idea of ministry certainly is not that of an elevated, power-wielding priesthood; rather, the New Testament term designates a servant who ministers as the Master did. We are now ready for the second question.

WHAT DOES THE MINISTRY DO?

John Knox, professor of New Testament at Union Theological Seminary in New York, in a study of the use of the word *minister*, says: "A minister (diakonos) of Christ is useful to Christ, assisting in the fulfillment of Christ's purposes in the world. A minister of the church is useful to the church, serving its members in all possible ways and contributing to the growth and effective functioning of the church itself."[5]

That ministry is directly related to God and His revelation *to* man and His will *for* man. Although ministry is more than preaching and proclamation, it does relate to a message. I see four important aspects in this.

1. There is a message from God of vital importance.
2. The message is committed to man for transmission.
3. The man who carries the message from God
   a. Must be a man of God,
   b. Must know what the message is, and
   c. Must engage actively in its proclamation.
4. The result of that ministry is evidenced in the growth of the church.

The first aspect deals with revelation and soteriology. The second deals with ecclesiology and particularly missiology. The third deals with theological education, and the last attests to the effectiveness of the message, the man, and his education. That is ministry.

It is obvious that two concepts have developed from the early use of the terms *doulos* and *diakonia*; and as a ship overlong at sea gets encrusted with barnacles, so both concepts have gathered extrabiblical accoutrements. The slave has become the master, whereas the ministry of the body has been taken away from the body and become the exclusive, guarded right of those with "holy orders." It is common for the congregation to excuse themselves from ministry and insist on the following three ideas:

1. The work of ministry is holy and the congregation should not take it upon themselves. Remember when the ark was about to fall over? One would certainly think that it should be supported, but not so. The one who put his hand on that holy work was punished. The laity is not to do the holy work of ministry.

2. We all have our gifts. The congregation's is to make money and pay the preacher to do the work. Why, if the congregation did the work, the pastor would not have a job!

3. God calls some to the harvest field, and woe be unto the man who enters the work without a call.

C. Peter Wagner lists seven things needed for a successful church. The first is a strong leader. But a strong leader does not do all the work. "*If the first vital sign of a growing church is a pastor who is using his gifts to lead his church into growth, the second is a well-mobilized laity.* One cannot function apart from the other any more than blood circulation and respiration can function apart from each other in the human body."[6]

Although I recognize a ministry that is unique and separate, I am also convinced that the church has been seriously hindered by a nonministering laity. Let me support that from H. A. Snyder's comment on the successful pastor as a superstar who outshines monogifted laymen:

> If the pastor is a superstar, then the church is an audience, not a body. I had read many times what the Bible says about the gifts of the Spirit. I never understood. I could not figure out why the whole thing really did not make any sense for the church *today*. It did not seem to fit. Could it really be that these words were written only for the early church, as some affirm?
>
> Then it struck me. These words are for the church in every age, but to the church today they seem superfluous. For we have got all the gifts organized. We do not need the Spirit (Dreadful thing to say!) to stir up gifts of ministry. We just need superstars to make the organization *Go*.
>
> So we depend on our structures and our superstars. . . . But the church of Jesus Christ cannot run on superstars, and God never intended that it should. . . .

God does not promise the church an affluence of superstars. But He does promise to provide all the necessary leadership through the gifts of the Spirit.[7]

The real key to effective ministry lies on the threshold of recognition today and needs to be thoroughly recognized and laid hold of to accomplish the great task that exists worldwide—*discipling the multitudes*. It is in that light that I insist on a theological education that *equips the ministry as enablers of the body*.

Ray Stedman, along with others who stress the ministry of the laity, has given us a renewed awareness of the body and what it does. He says that the radically changed life results in a ministry that

> does not require a formal or stylized presentation nor a special place or time. It is not restricted to those who are ordained or are "in the ministry." Every person who has experienced true Christianity is already in the ministry because he or she possesses what others desperately need. It is this abundant ministry, available to all, which the apostle now describes: "All this is from God, who through Christ reconciled us to Himself and gave us the ministry of reconciliation; that is, God was in Christ reconciling the world to Himself, not counting their trespasses against them, and entrusting to us the message of reconciliation."[8]

That ministry of reconciliation is the natural result of the overflowing life; and in that ministry the whole body (the church) exercises its several gifts.

Usually the minister-laity relationship is represented as a dichotomy, in this manner:

The minister and his work	**The layman and his work**

It is assumed that a definite, uncrossable division separates the two. Some thinking ecclesiastics react to that by affirming that there is a biblically based, God-ordained, historically accepted division, but that the laity have been neglected. They suggest that the solution may be found in shifting the work balance line to indicate a more involved laity, represented like this:

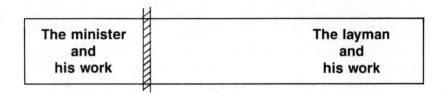

Others would argue that the relationship would be better represented by a vertical model that not only indicates quantity of activity but also gives a representation of authority and supremacy.

Such a model recognizes that the laity are to be involved and suggests that consideration be given to what constitutes the activities of each of the two groups. Activities of the ministers are limited to activities of ministry status, and "suitable" activities for the laity are naturally of a lower nature. In such a model, status is maintained in the designation of jobs and does not allow us to see ministry as the function of the body.

In matching duties with laity-ministry positions we could also think of conditioning that creates matched pairs such as nail-hammer, shirt-tie, table-chair, and ordained man-ministry. Again the conclusion is a historically conditioned fallacy. What should be the matched pair combination involving ordained minister and laity?

A very helpful model indicating in a fresh way where ministry is shared by clergy and laity can be made by avoiding a rigid dichotomy and allowing an in-between area shared equally.

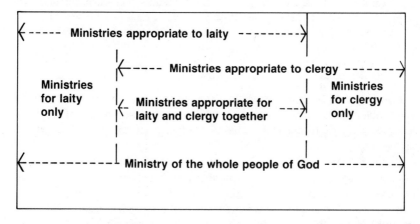

THE MINISTRY OF THE WHOLE BODY

A dichotomy in the church certainly was not true for the first two hundred years of its history. "In the discussion of the ministry in the New Testament four factors must be borne in mind: (1) All ministry centers in Jesus Christ; (2) the entire Christian community is active in ministry; (3) the ministry is given by God and is exercised through the spontaneous use of special gifts; and (4) special ministries are needed for specific situations in an evolving society."[9]

We are not trying to say that there is no place for leaders; rather, we are saying that leaders have a function as a part of the body.

Although we are basically searching for theological education that prepares people *for* ministry, it is obvious that we must continue, as we have been doing, to consider who does ministry and to urge a greater acceptance of the idea that the whole church (laity *and* clergy) perform that ministry. to support that emphasis we refer to the problem as seen by Ralph D. Winter:

> In Latin America there are by the latest estimates 74,953 Protestant congregations. Since there are an average of at least two (perhaps three) "preaching points" for each of these congregations, this means there are a minimum of 150,000 men of pastoral gifts, probably 90% of which seriously lack further training. But if only 100,000 of them need ministerial training, this is a massive, urgent challenge. To meet this challenge, there are sixty seminaries with a total enrollment of one thousand plus 300 Bible institutes with a total enrollment of some 12,000. Even assuming these students were all to become pastors, or better still, were mainly men in the group of 100,000 who are already on the job, we would still be backlogged for fifteen years in meeting the need by conventional methods. And this assumes that the movement would stand still, needing no more pastors than it needs right now.[10]

Coupling the earlier references to a ministering laity and the Latin American problem just mentioned leads one to recognize the success of the Pentecostals in their informal approaches to theological education and their use of lay workers.

One non-Pentecostal church in Argentina emphasized professional leaders' training to the point of training more leaders than could be hired by its churches, thus showing a lack of emphasis on planting new churches and slow use of laity rather than adequate preparation of appropriate leadership. Arno W. Enns reports that "this strong emphasis on the training of professionals, however, has led to a concomitant neglect of lay leadership and the overdevelopment of the specialized clergy. This characteristic should be compared with the Pentecostal emphasis on lay leadership. It is the effective use of lay leaders which has proved to be the key to the expansion of the Church throughout Latin America, not the paid clergy, important and crucial as their work has been."[11]

In setting out ten keys to church growth in Argentina, Enns lists as number four the mobilization of the total body and says: "Those churches in which the laymen are responsible for, and actively participate in, the different ministries of the congregation find a 'bridge of God' out into the world and back into the community of Christians. Where this has taken place among the churches in Argentina, there has been multiplied growth far beyond what one professional leader would be able to produce and maintain on his own."[12]

How Do We Train for the Ministry?

Theological education must train ministers to accept their place in the body. As TEE has moved the training concept from training *for* the ministry to training *in* ministry, so we need a move from training that fits a minister for a traditional priestly office to training that is designed to give him the tools, insights, knowledge, and spiritual formation needed so that he can prepare the members of the body for their ministry. That will certainly include a rethinking of ecclesiology, ministry, and theological education in regard to both nonformal modes and curriculum content and structure.

We must recognize as imperative the need to reshape theological education as training *in* ministry to equip the body *for* ministry in accord with Ephesians 4:11-12: "And these were his gifts: some to be apostles, some prophets, some evangelists, some pastors and teachers, to equip God's people for work in his service [ministry], to the building up of the body of Christ" (*New English Bible*).

We may and should ask whether the courses being taught in theological school prepare for that kind of ministry; and if the subject ranks a place in the curriculum, we should ask if it is taught by a person who demonstrates ministry *in* his life? Teachers in theological schools must be men of God. Augustine said of Ambrose: "To Milan I came, to Ambrose the Bishop, known to the whole world as among the best of men, Thy devout servant; whose eloquent discourse did then plentifully dispense unto Thy people the flour of Thy wheat, the gladness of Thy oil, and the sober inebriation of Thy wine. To him was I unknowing led by Thee, that by him I might knowingly be led to Thee."[13]

Lest I be indicted for rejecting proper theological studies, I appeal to a man from church history who was both scholar and minister, John Wesley. He early had to face the rejection of his ministers because they had neither "proper" theological training nor "proper" ecclesiastical orders. When accused of making use of the ignorant and illiterate, Wesley replied that the Methodists "do not allow the 'most ignorant' to preach but such as

145

1) are truly alive to God, with love to God and to man,

2) have a competent knowledge of the word, and

3) have given proof they are called of God."[14]

Wesley was aware that a man needs to know the Word of God. He also knew the difference between schooling and knowledge, and said of one of his preachers, John Cownly, "His learning was confined though his knowledge was extensive."[15] Wesley insisted on his workers' being "alive to God" and having "proof they are called." He emphasized the necessity of man's having acquired endowments as well as having studied an impressive list of subjects including: what the ministry is, Scripture, original languages, history, science (including logic, philosophy, geometry), the early fathers (including Chrysostom and Jerome), the world of man and his life, common science, and good breeding (including propriety of behavior and how to speak properly).[16]

Wesley certainly cannot be accused of anti-intellectualism, and my purpose for rehearsing those matters is not to disregard formal studies. Rather, I want to emphasize how essential it is to keep in mind the simple pragmatic question: After you know it, what are you going to do with it? Wesley went beyond the academics of the classroom to learning by doing. His was a training *in* ministry. In a letter regarding true ministry, he gave this qualification for effectiveness: "Give me one hundred preachers who fear nothing but sin and I care not a straw whether they be clergymen or laymen, such alone will shake the gates of hell and set up the kingdom of heaven upon earth."[17]

THE MINISTER'S PRIME TASK

As has been seen, ministry is doing. The ministry is done by the body, "whether they be clergymen or laymen." An ordained elite is not set aside to do the work of ministry; rather, the clergy should equip the body to minister. One of the benefits of TEE has been that the local leader is given skills that can help him become an enabler of the laity. In theological education we must have a biblical concept of ministry and develop a training system that prepares leaders to be such enablers.

It may seem trite to say that leaders should lead, but our problem is that many do not. Perhaps our method of training does not equip people to be leaders. That lack in our method of training may come from error in our theology of the church and ministry. The purpose of theological education is to produce leaders—men who show the way and take the way. Institutions cannot *make* leaders, but they should certainly be expected to try to provide their students with skill in ministerial leadership. I have heard management experts say that you can always tell a leader because he has followers! We need to observe such presently existing leaders who have followers and ask ourselves:

1. What is successful ministry?

2. What should a leader know, what must he be, and what must he be able to do to perform successful ministry?

3. What educational process is needed to change a novice from nonexistent, inadequate, or faulty knowing, being, and doing to successful knowing, being, and doing in performance of ministry?

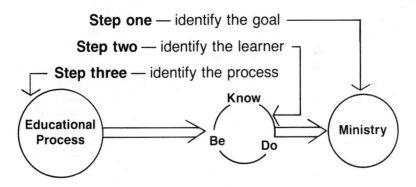

In Africa I sensed that the key to dynamic church life and growth among the Ndebele of Rhodesia was the local leader. But the system of theological education carried around the world is the Western model of the seminary with its emphasis on theological content. That approach has not been fully effective in producing pastors for churches even in the United States, and perhaps the renewed concern for leadership may now bring pressures on the seminaries to reconsider their curricula in light of job needs. Such reconsideration coupled with the growing emphasis on the involvement of the laity in ministry and the function of body life in the church may assist in renewal in theological education. Because the key to a successful church is a leader who motivates the whole body to ministry, it is that concern toward which theological education must plan its program.

The ministry *is* the work of the whole body; but, as we note from Ephesians, there are those who, although they are part of the body, have a distinct work of leadership and the ministry of teaching so as to equip the body for the ministry. That is the premise of Ephesians 4, which I diagram as follows (see also Rom. 12 and 1 Cor. 12):

God's gifts to the church:

Apostles
Prophets
Evangelists
Pastor-teachers

Christ
the
Head

For the equipping
of the body:

Wisdom
Knowledge
Faith
Healing
Miracles
Prophecy
Discernment
Tongues
Interpretation
Teaching
Helps
Administration
Giving

So that the body can do the
work of the ministry:

1. Maturation
2. Worship
3. Service
4. Witness

Theological education needs our serious attention, for the task of world evangelism will only be accomplished as the enablers of the body move from the center of the stage to the sidelines and let the ministry of the whole church function in all its God-inspired fullness.

Discussion Questions

1. Discuss "the work of the ministry" in your church. Who does it? What does the ministry consist of? How would it be diagramed graphically (see pp. 142-43) What changes would you like to see?
2. Differentiate between training *for* the ministry and training *in* the ministry. In what way will that distinction affect a program of theological education? How is training *in* ministry related to church growth?
3. What makes a ministry successful? How is success measured?

1. Hans Küng, *Why Priests? A Proposal for a New Church Ministry* (Garden City, N.Y.: Doubleday, 1972), p. 83.
2. Seward Hiltner, *Ferment in the Ministry* (New York: Abingdon, 1969), p. 35.
3. Nathan M. Pusey and Charles L. Taylor, *Ministry for Tomorrow* (New York: Seabury, 1967), p. 119.
4. John V. Taylor, "Preparing the Ordinand for Mission," *International Review of Missions, Special Issue on Theological Education* 56 (1967):147.
5. H. Richard Niebuhr and Daniel D. Williams, eds., *The Ministry in Historical Perspective* (New York: Harper & Row, 1956), p. 2.
6. C. Peter Wagner, *Your Church Can Grow* (Glendale, Calif.: Regal, 1976), p. 69.
7. H. A. Snyder, *The Problem of Wineskins* (Downers Grove, Ill.: InterVarsity, 1975), pp. 83-84.
8. Ray C. Stedman, *Authentic Christianity* (Waco, Tex.: Word, 1976), p. 162.
9. Erwin L. Lueker, *Change and the Church* (St. Louis: Concordia, 1969), p. 118.
10. Donald A. McGavran, *Church Growth Bulletin, vols.* 1-5 (Pasadena, Calif.: William Carey Library, 1969), p. 242.
11. Arno W. Enns, *Man, Milieu, and Mission in Argentina* (Grand Rapids: Eerdmans, 1971), p. 94.
12. Ibid p. 215.
13. Augustine, *The Confessions of Saint Augustine* (New York: Liveright, 1943), p. 103.
14. A. B. Lawson, *John Wesley and the Christian Minister* (London: SPCK, 1963), p. 100.
15. G. Holden Pike, *Wesley and His Preachers* (London: T. Fisher Unwin, 1903), p. 34.
16. John Wesley, *The Works of the Reverend John Wesley, A. M.* (London: John Mason, 1841), 10:463ff.
17. John Wesley, *The Letters of the Reverend John Wesley,* ed. J. Telford (London: Epworth, 1931), 6:272.

Case Studies

9

Contextualization of Theological Education in Indonesia

Avery T. Willis, Jr.

In January 1974 the Indonesian Baptist Theological Seminary opened six regional branches with a total of forty-six teaching centers and an enrollment of over four hundred students. The seminary's purpose is to provide theological education designed specifically for Indonesian spiritual leaders of varying educational backgrounds, abilities, and opportunities for study. Its goal is to educate and train leaders who are presently serving in their local churches, in order to equip them to serve effectively in the context of their own situation.

The term *contextualization* has grown in popularity in theological circles until it has become one of the basic goals in the theological world. Many theological schools in the emerging countries are investigating what contextualization means in contrast to the educational models imported from Europe and America. The tide of development in the emerging countries motivates

AVERY T. WILLIS, JR. (Th.D., Southwestern Baptist Theological Seminary) is supervisor of the Adult Section of the Church Training Department of the Sunday School Board of the Southern Baptist Convention. From 1964 to 1978 Dr. Willis was a missionary under the Foreign Mission Board of the Southern Baptist Convention. He served as president of the Indonesian Baptist Theological Seminary.

them to create a theology that applies to their culture, situation, aspirations, and thought patterns without compromising the biblical revelation.

The first innovations toward contextualization of theological education by the Indonesian Baptist Theological Seminary were initiated in 1971, following three years of research that revealed traumatic changes had occurred in the Indonesian churches since 1965.

- A national political upheaval, including an abortive communist coup and the macabre deaths of approximately four hundred thousand Indonesians, had altered the religious life of the nation.[1]
- A religious revival had resulted in two million baptisms in the churches between 1965 and 1971.[2]
- That influx of new Christians forced the churches to rethink their church structures, their concept of the ministry, and the function of theological education.
- Five major denominations working primarily with the Javanese inaugurated innovative leadership training programs in order to meet the needs of the new congregations that had sprung up throughout the countryside.
- Baptist churches had doubled their membership and in the process had shifted their sociological center to the Javanese in rural areas.

The surveys revealed that the Baptist churches had not made many attempts to indigenize their structure, theology, or methods imported from North America.

The Indonesian Baptist Mission accepted the responsibility for the imported program of church life that was both foreign to and inappropriate for the Javanese in the rural areas. Several factors made it clear that the best interests of the churches were not being served by the seminary. Seminary enrollment was increasing dramatically in the wake of nationwide revival movements, but the students were being trained to perpetuate a style of church life based on American theology and methodology. Subsidy had raised their expectations for an assured position, pastoring a fully-equipped and functioning church, on graduation. Now there were more graduates than positions of that kind offered. They were producing very few new churches that could grow and sustain themselves in the local environment. The dormitory pattern had extracted the students from their culture, partially Westernized them, and made them unable or unwilling to return to the villages from which they had come. The Western-style church insulated both pastors and members from the indigenous forms and natural lines of communication in the culture. The students had become victims, although willingly, of an instructional approach that made them dependent on foreign funds and expertise and which, at best, equipped them only to sustain an American model that was not viable in the culture.

In order to meet the overwhelming opportunities in Indonesia, the Mission instituted a "New Pattern of Work," which placed the priority on beginning thousands of churches in homes, led by local leaders. The pattern was designed to encourage local leaders to develop biblical theology, church patterns, and life-styles that were in keeping with the needs and thought patterns of the Indonesians, thereby aiding church growth.

The contextualization of church life demanded the contextualization of theological education. To effect that change, the Mission voted to discontinue the existing program of theological education and to redeploy the professors to the various provinces to develop a program of theological education from the grass roots up.

The Indonesian Baptist Union, organized by the Baptist churches in 1971, protested the proposed changes, so the official opening of the expanded theological education program was postponed until 1974. The Mission's original proposal was modified to continue theological education at the resident seminary using a revised curriculum and an accelerated schedule. Seventy-five more students were graduated from the residence program by 1973. The decision to phase out the original program was primarily a decision to begin a search for what was appropriate in the Indonesian context and to find a way for the seminary to help implement it. It was only the first step in a pilgrimage that was to lead to ever-unfolding innovations including inaugurating a new residence program in 1979 that incorporated the benefits derived from eight years of contextualization.

The search for a different educational methodology demanded a look at a trial project in TEE (theological education by extension) that the Mission had started earlier in East Java. The Mission did not immediately adopt TEE: in fact, it pointedly avoided naming any kind of methodology.

The seminary faculty and board used those two and one-half years, while phasing out the former program, to study the educational needs of the leaders of the churches in Indonesia. They examined the "rice roots" and began to discover indigenous Indonesian expressions for biblical truths. They experimented with new forms of church life that Indonesians could reproduce. They concluded that a broadened outreach of theological education could help mature leaders serve their people in their own locales. They began to wrestle with the theological questions that were arising in the churches rather than addressing themselves to imported theological problems that had arisen in American and European traditions.

In short, they began to hunger for the sort of theological education that would serve the churches and produce the kind of graduates the churches needed. Such graduates would identify with the people and be willing to live on the level of those served. They would need a strong scriptural base and an intimate knowledge of the culture in order to participate in the formulation of a theology, both authentic and biblical, in the present Indonesian context.

The base design of the seminary includes the following statements, which sum up its convictions about the thrust of theological education:

1. All the people of God are called to be priests, servants, and sons of God in building the Kingdom of God.
2. God has given apostles, prophets, evangelists, pastors and teachers to His Church to equip all its members to serve.
3. The purpose of theological education is to educate and train church leaders who in turn equip church members to worship, fellowship, study, serve, evangelize, and start churches.
4. Theological education is provided only for spiritual leaders who have already proven themselves in ministry in their local churches.
5. Students are received on the basis of their faith, faithfulness, ability to bear responsibility, and the exercise of spiritual gifts in their ministries, not on factors that have arisen in Christian history to divide God's people into classes such as: time (fulltime or part time), money (paid or voluntary), education (general or theological), status (clergy or laity), calling (specific or general).

CONTEXTUALIZATION OF LOCATION

The most obvious meaning of contextualization relates to the location in which the student receives his theological education. The contextualization approach takes theological education to the student, instead of extracting him from his environment. Our former resident program took students out of their indigenous culture and Westernized them to such an extent during their four years of theological training that they did not want to return to their villages to serve after graduation. We now emphasize training leaders who are already serving in their churches, many of whom find it impossible to attend a resident seminary because of family, church, or work responsibilities. The student's contact with the world makes the contextualization of theology natural. Eighty-six percent are employed in secular work in addition to their church ministries; the other 14 percent consists of housewives (10 percent) and fully supported pastors (4 percent). Their work takes them into all areas of Indonesian life: 19 percent are farmers, 17 percent government workers, 16 percent white collar businessmen, 13 percent schoolteachers, 5 percent merchants, and the rest are peddlers, soldiers, university students, professional people, and so on. Sixty-four percent are married, and over half the students have families.

Expenses for the school and the student are less when he studies in his own context. He also learns to depend on God and his local church for financial support rather than on foreign funds. Of course, he faces some disadvantages studying in context, such as distractions and the prolongation of his education. Although his seminary education could last from seven to fifteen years, he has the advantage of self-pacing and instituting lifetime study habits in the environment in which he will live and serve.

CONTEXTUALIZATION FOR STUDENTS

The student is the focal point in our theological education program. He learns by an inductive, situational methodology, which originates with the needs of the student rather than with the content the professor wants to teach. Questions raised by the students in their cultural and church contexts become the foundation for the writing of programmed textbooks that provide relevant answers based on biblical and historical principles and practical experience.

We currently teach on four educational levels in order to meet the students at their point of need.

- *The highest education level,* M.Div. and B.Th. *(Tinggi)* is for students who already have a high school or university education.
- *The diploma level (Menengah Atas)* teaches students who have completed junior high school.

- *The certificate level (Menengah)* serves those who have finished elementary school.
- *A Christian workers level (Dasar)* endeavors to teach those who do not qualify for the other levels, that is, they have less than a sixth-grade education, have served less than two years in their church, or are less than twenty-three years of age.

Graduate levels, leading to the Th.M. and D.Min. degrees are offered in cooperation with the Asia Baptist Graduate Theological Seminary. Among active students, 31 are enrolled in the M.Div. program, 123 in the B.Th. program, 76 in the diploma program, 43 in the certificate program, and 135 in the Christian workers program. Of those in the Christian workers program, 104 should eventually fulfill the enrollment requirements and move up to their respective educational levels.

The focus for study is their ministry in the local church. A written fieldwork report is required in each course. Each course involves the student in learning activities in his church and environment, with a view to producing vibrant churches. The programmed textbooks relate to his practical ministry. Projects are assigned and must be reported on. The regional director interviews each student each year to review his practical ministry.

In this new system, the student learns in a natural situation where he can immediately apply what he has learned in his local church. He is not taught a "body of theories" or "a system of theology," which he should later attempt to adapt to his situation, but he learns to apply theology in his context as he serves.

The students double up in their ministries as preachers (25 percent), evangelists (30 percent), Bible teachers or Sunday school teachers (61 percent), and other positions of leadership (58 percent). Over one hundred serve as primary leaders of their churches. Of the churches served, 41 percent are urban, 41 percent are rural, and 18 percent suburban.

CONTEXTUALIZATION OF CONTENT

The presence of the student in his context demands content directly related to his social and cultural situation. Programmed textbooks and weekly seminar sessions deal with specific religious, cultural, and social problems encountered by the student. The programmed textbooks are written in the Indonesian language, tested on representative students, and revised until they meet the needs of that particular educational level. The weekly seminar sessions in the teaching centers allow the teachers to give more on-the-spot, personal attention to the individual student than they could in larger classes. Special projects, regional quarterly retreats, and an annual National Study Week at the resident seminary involve the students in meaningful group experiences. A built-in system of feedback from students enables the seminary to continually adjust to meet their needs.

Often the theological education by extension movement has simply diffused the imported theological content that was previously taught in the classical seminary out into myriad teaching centers. Our emphasis on the student and his context, more than on the theological content, has resulted in a new perspective of curriculum. We began our curriculum revision by describing the kind of knowledge, skills, and attitudes needed by our graduates to serve effectively in the Indonesian context. That resulted in the formulation of five basic goals included in the statement of purpose:

> The purpose of the Indonesian Baptist Theological Seminary is to educate and train Baptist leaders who are evidencing spiritual gifts, in order that they will be able to serve Christ effectively by:
> 1—understanding and using the Bible
> 2—maintaining a growing spiritual life
> 3—communicating Christian truths
> 4—planting and shepherding churches, and
> 5—equipping the people of God to serve

Those goals, the student-centered perspective, and the Indonesian context shaped the new curriculum. But we had not gone far enough, according to Dr. LeRoy Ford, who visited Indonesia to assist us in educational methodology. He suggested that those goals be broken down into specific behavorial objectives. The description of the graduate was then written in terms of approximately one hundred fifty specific objectives, in the cognitive, psychomotor, and affective domains, leading to the attainment of the five basic goals. Those specific objectives demanded a further revision of our ''new'' curriculum, which had been too content-oriented.

The specific objectives are attained through a curriculum of sixty courses in a quarter system, designed to meet particular objectives the sum of which leads the student to attain the stated goals. Each course has an additional fifty to one hundred intermediate objectives. Even the Bible courses are studied from the perspective of specific behavorial objectives. For instance, the primary goal of the course on 1 Corinthians is: "that the student will be able to overcome nine kinds of church problems using the principles enunciated by Paul in 1 Corinthians and then teach the essence of the lessons to another church leader."

One of the evangelism courses has this goal: "The student will be able to differentiate between the basic Christian beliefs and the beliefs of animists and Moslems in Indonesia, to find points of contact between these beliefs, and to devise methods of approach and witness to people with animistic and Islamic backgrounds."

The emphasis is placed on goals that are important, lasting, practical, and personal, that can be passed on as the student equips the people of God. The goals are reached through a program of planned learning.

A study of the psychology of learning and the discovery of new educational technologies developed in recent years shed much light on how to achieve our goals and objectives. Once the seminary committed itself to achieve specific goals and objectives, it was obligated to provide resources for the learning experiences. The initial dramatic changes in the *form* of theological education have given way to emerging changes in the process of instruction, which in turn has led to further changes in the nature of the *content*. Particular emphasis has been placed on making theological education life-centered, practically oriented, biblically relevant, and educationally sound, using various models of instructional design. The goal is to provide dynamic, interactive, and relevant learning experiences that stimulate the development of ministers and equip them to serve effectively in all kinds of real-life situations.

One method being developed and used by the seminary to contextualize theology is the Life-Situation Learning Model. A life-situation analysis of the student (largely a guided self-discovery) reveals a problem and its context. It (1) describes the conflict inherent in the problem, (2) identifies the issues involved in the conflict, (3) discovers the values reflected in the issues, (4) explores the cultural and sociological context that conditioned the values, and (5) determines the importance of the problem to the student in the context of his ministry.

The results of the analysis are used to assist the student to: (1) face a choice between issues and values embodied in a specific problem that is important to him, (2) discover the options and weigh the advantages and disadvantages of each, (3) choose a solution from the available options, (4) experience the application of the solution in the context of home, church, community, or society, (5) evaluate the experience by interacting with other students, professors, and the people to whom he ministers, (6) teach someone else what he has learned while adapting it to the new learning environment, and (7) plan further projects to complement his knowledge, self-understanding, and development.

The Taxonomy of Educational Objectives[3] has been helpful to both authors and teachers in leading students to attain cognitive, psychomotor, and affective goals through various kinds and levels of learning experiences. Continual training and revision are an integral part of enabling authors to write effective textbooks.

The student studies each programmed textbook approximately five hours per week, prior to attending a weekly seminar with other students in his area. During that meeting, he explores the meanings, implications, and applications of the material under the direction of a seminary professor. The programmed texts, equivalent to 400-page textbooks, lead the students step-by-step to accomplish the stated objectives through varied learning activities. But we are convinced that the teacher is indispensable in theological education and that seminars, retreats, and practical projects are essential to attain the affective as well as the cognitive and psychomotor goals.

The most difficult problem faced to date has been the producing of the programmed texts. Forty-one of the proposed 120 books were published during the first three years, providing eight courses a year on four educational levels. Thirty-seven writers, twenty of whom are Indonesians, have written or are in the process of writing 14 textbooks each year. Each writer designs specific objectives to reach the goals for his course and has them approved by the seminary staff before programming the textbook. At least ten people are involved in the process of aiding each writer in matters of content, format, and language. The books are tested several times with individual students from the designated levels and, when time allows, with groups in order to discover where revisions are needed. If a student is unable to answer a question or pass a test, it is considered the author's responsibility to revise the book until any competent student of the designated level can master the material presented. It takes part-time writers at least one and one-half years to prepare 1 programmed text.

In order to contextualize theology in the Indonesian situation, no programmed textbooks from other countries were used during the first two and one-half years. We are now experimenting with contextualizing selected courses from other countries in the Third World.

It is obvious that the basic methodology is borrowed from Western educational technology, but we continue to make adaptations to the Indonesian context. We are emphasizing planned learning, rather than limiting ourselves to a strictly programmed format, which does not always lend itself to all phases of theological education. The contextualization of methodology is complicated by the fact that no significant research on how Indonesians learn has been done. The Indonesian public school system is built on a model of learning imported from the Netherlands and more recently the United States.

Unknown to us when we started, the Indonesian government has become aware of the need to revise its educational system. The minister of education has cited four major problem areas: broadening the base for public education, increasing the quality of education, making education relevant to modern development, and improving its efficiency and effectiveness. In 1975 a new curriculum based on the Developmental Instructional System was introduced. That system parallels the system of educational technology used by the seminary. A "Taxonomy Manual" produced by the seminary has been requested and distributed to 200 high school teachers in central Java.

CONTEXTUALIZATION OF PERSONNEL

One of our most serious shortcomings in the former seminary program was the failure to provide adequate training programs for the development of Indonesian educators. The contextualization program has necessitated the development of national leadership. The seminary now has Indonesians in the positions of dean, supervisor of writers, editor of programmed literature, business administrator, and assistant regional director.* The Indonesian staff conducts programmed literature workshops and helps surpervise the development of textbooks. Nineteen graduates of the former program are teachers in the regional centers, and twenty are involved in writing textbooks. We missionary educators and administrators have specific devolution plans and are training our Indonesian counterparts to do our jobs. In addition to in-service training, selected leaders of the seminary receive assistance in obtaining further formal education. The goal is that Indonesians will be able to administrate the entire program of theological education for Baptists in Indonesia.

CONCLUSIONS

We have learned many lessons since 1971 when we launched the contextualization program. Subsequent evaluations indicate that students in the contextualized theological program can receive the same high quality of theological education as those in resident seminaries, plus added advantages of contextualization already mentioned. Personal renewal and spiritual revival resulting in church growth have occurred among a large number of students.

We are convinced that theological education exists to serve churches rather than itself. It is an educational arm of the Body of Christ and originates, flourishes, and finds its fulfillment within the framework and the life of the churches. The nature of the New Testament church demands the ministry of teaching and training. Those who teach and train others must be trained first. A contextualized seminary fulfills that inherent need. That does not prevent—in fact it can enhance and increase—the effectiveness of a resident theological graduate school. Complete contextualization must move toward the liberation from the culture of the sending country, domination by missionaries, and dependence on foreign funds. The Indonesian Baptist Theological Seminary has a long way to go to attain those goals, but it has begun and with God's help will continue to contextualize theological education in Indonesia.

Discussion Questions

1. Define and discuss the meaning of the term *contextualization*.
2. How is theological education affected by the location and setting in which the student studies?
3. In what way does the articulation of specific behavioral objectives for each

course assist the student in applying what he is learning to the particular real-life situation in which he is working?

4. In what way is contextualization of personnel a necessary component in the development of a theological education program overseas? Is that basic premise on the mission field also applicable to us in the United States? How?

1. Justus Van der Kroof, *Indonesia Since Sukarno* (Singapore: Asia Pacific Press, 1971), p. 14. The estimates of the number of deaths vary from the 87,000 officially reported to the 1,000,000 reported by a team of University of Indonesia students commissioned by the army.
2. Avery Willis, Jr., *Indonesian Revival: Why Two Million Came to Christ* (South Pasadena: William Carey Library, 1977), p. 9.
3. Benjamin S. Bloom, ed., *Taxonomy of Educational Objectives,* Handbook I, Cognitive Domain (New York: David McKay, 1956); David R. Krathevohl, et al., *Taxonomy of Educational Objectives,* Handbook II, Affective Domain (New York: David McKay, 1964).

*In 1979 an Indonesian was elected to share the top leadership post, by a board of trustees made up of an equal number of Indonesians and missionaries. The board works under the direction of the national Union of Indonesian Baptist Churches.

10

Let's Multiply Churches Through TEE

George Patterson

Editor's note: Here is a missionary's report of one of the most significant developments in TEE (theological education by extension). George Patterson's innovative "extension chains" coupled with the preparation and use of semiprogrammed materials in a rural area produced twenty-five new congregations in a three-year period!

Patterson has pioneered in TEE for semiliterate students. His work is at a level that to my knowledge no one else has yet attempted. This chapter is not mere theory. It has been hammered out in the mountains and valleys of northern Honduras. It is the result of constant revision and evaluation to fit the needs on his own field and its unique cultural context. But many of his basic principles have a universal application to all mission situations, and I heartily commend them to readers for study and consideration.

Do you have segments of the population within your area of responsibility that still lack active, growing churches? If so, you may want to add to your present education program an *extension chain*. Evangelism and education can be integrated so that both ministries reinforce each other in the same extension center. Simply program your students' studies and activities to initiate and sustain a self-multiplying chain of new churches. First let us define the terms used in such a program:

Mother church: a congregation that mobilizes men in another locality to raise up their own church and pastor it.

Daughter church: a congregation raised up within an extension chain by a mother church.

Extension center: a place other than a resident seminary or institute where classes are held (usually by one or more churches) to train and mobilize Christian workers for immediate service.

Subcenter: an extension center operated by a *student* of another center.

Extension chain: the process of church reproduction in which a mother church with an extension center starts one or more daughter churches that in turn become extension centers and start more churches. For example, the Baptist church in Olanchito, Honduras, raised up several daughter churches through its extension program. One of them, in Jocon, raised up four granddaughter churches. The granddaughter church in San Lorenzo, in turn, is raising up other churches nearby. It took from between three months to two years to add each link to the chain.

The links are not individual witnesses; they are congregations. The most effective unit for spiritual reproduction is the local church. An individual should witness for Christ as an arm of his own congregation. Making obedient disciples as demanded by the Great Commission requires a team effort. Persons with different spiritual gifts work together. The *body* reproduces itself. The daughter church inherits the seed of reproduction from the mother church to produce granddaughter churches.

Dead-end link: an extension-chain church that fails to become a mother church in its turn.

Lay pastor: a volunteer, part-time worker locally trained and licensed by his own congregation to baptize, officiate at the Lord's Supper, and serve as pastor. He lacks the formal training normally required for ordained pastors and does not use the title "Reverend."

Reteachable materials: self-teaching textbooks made especially for the in-service training of a pastor who reteaches the materials to his church or to his own extension students, who may then reteach the same studies the following week to their own students in another subcenter.

Principal of an extension chain: the first teacher in an extension chain. Both educator and church planter, the principal must initiate and direct the flow of reteachable materials, ideas, and activities. He may be the only teacher in the chain with previous theological education. His students become extension teachers under his direction as soon as they have begun raising up their first daughter churches. For example, the principal of the chain in Honduras teaches 4 student-workers in 2 centers. Those men reteach the same materials to another 35 men in 18 subcenters who in turn are reaching over 100 student-workers in more than 80 congregations (43 of which are fully organized churches). Some of those pastors-in-training teach as many as 25 men in more remote villages. The chain provides pastoral training in 30 congregations. To make the outer links grow and multiply, there must be edifying teaching all the way along the chain. That teaching helps the older churches to keep growing too.

Student-worker: a Christian worker who receives in-service training on the job. He does not study just to prepare himself for the future; he puts his extension studies into immediate practice.

FIVE SIMPLE STEPS YOU CAN TAKE IN STARTING AN EXTENSION CHAIN

1. VERIFY YOUR QUALIFICATIONS

a) Pastoral experience. The principal supervises the in-service training of pastors all along the chain. The principal must have a pastor's heart and experience. If you lack pastoral experience, work closely with a pastor.

b) Extension know-how. Knowledge and experience in education by extension is essential to success. You must do some in-service training in addition to securing or writing reteachable materials geared to both your student's progress and his church's needs.

c) Evangelistic vision. You must keep the churches multiplying. God wants

His church to take root in every town and neighborhood in your field of responsibility. A healthy, obedient church is like a growing plant "whose seed is in itself." It *has* to grow and multiply. That is her nature, built into her by her Creator. Every teacher in the chain must have that vision.

d) Willingness to work with the local churches. You and your students must be authorized by your own churches to raise up new churches. God does not use self-appointed apostles or self-ordained pastors. Each student-worker must acknowledge that it is his church that sends him and not he himself. His church reproduces herself in the daughter church, not he himself. He is only a channel between the mother and daughter churches, through which the Holy Spirit communicates the gospel in human words and love.

e) Responsible leadership. Someone must visit and observe regularly all the works in the chain in order to counsel and in order to prepare reteachable materials for current needs.

2. MAKE WORKABLE PLANS

a) Start with the local church. Let the existing congregation feel part and parcel of the program from the beginning. Work out details together so that the initiation and implementation become theirs. The local church must approve, support, and participate in the plans.

b) Define your field of responsibility. You and every one of your student-teachers after you must define in exact terms his own field of responsibility. Draw a map and identify those segments of the society, geographical and social, for which God has made you responsible. It may be one town, or an area with several new and struggling churches, or a minority group within a larger society, or a very large field with many, many segments of population that have no churches.

c) Set specific targets. State your goals in definite, realistic terms. The ultimate objective of the Great Commission is a congregation of obedient disciples in every town and neighborhood in your field of responsibility. That prior conviction forces you to plan clear strategy. If your plans are not crystal clear, the churches you raise up will probably be dead-end links. Discuss the plans with local church leaders and student-teachers. Have faith in God's unlimited grace and aim for a chain reaction of church growth and multiplication that continues like a forest fire, generating its own heat as it spreads.

168

d) Elaborate immediate steps. As a principal, ask yourself: How will a mother church train the workers in the daughter church? Will they come to the mother church for extension classes? Or will the teacher go to the daughter church? If your field of responsibility is too large or socially complex to be reached with one chain, you will have to train other principals. Such large fields must be divided into sectors small enough to be reached from one strategically located center in each one. Establish churches first in those strategic locations, to serve as future extension centers. Break your plans down into easy, workable steps. Fit them into your time and budget.

3. RAISE UP THE FIRST DAUGHTER CHURCH YOURSELF

a) Make personal contacts in the new locality. You will go yourself to help start the first link in the chain. Set the example. But take with you some believer who has close friends or relatives in the new locality. Do not use special campaign methods, public invitations, loudspeakers, special tract campaigns, or any other gimmick until you and all your students have fully mastered the fundamentals of personal, effective witnessing. Each witness presents Christ first to his own family and friends (or to the family and friends of some believer who accompanies him).

b) Matriculate qualified students. Continue evangelizing until you have several men baptized. Then matriculate one or two of them, after they have started witnessing. In extension chains men are trained *in* their work, not *for* it. Limit the matriculation to those men who are actively obedient to Christ's commands. One or two is best. More than four will result in another passive Sunday school class. In each class you must deal with the details of each man's church work; you cannot do that with a crowd. Nor will a student take full responsibility for the work if he shares it with many others.

Do *not* matriculate single young men for an extension chain. You will have a dead-end "preaching point" with mainly women and children unless the leaders of a new work are local, mature family men of the type recommended in 1 Timothy 3:1-7.

You may have to teach your student to read. Do not hesitate to train a humble, uneducated peasant if he is typical of his group. Just be sure that he has the respect of his neighbors. Such men make the best lay pastors for people in his social group. They identify. They also make the best extension *teachers* for training other lay pastors of the same social class. That is how the Baptist and Methodist churches grew and multiplied so on the old American frontier.

c) Mobilize the new student-worker to raise up his own church and pastor it. Let him direct his new congregation from the very beginning (Acts 14:23). For that you must spend at least half of every class discussing the church work of your student: his experiences witnessing, his travels, his problems, his plans, and so forth. Hear his complete report and write down plans for his next period's work. Gear your teaching to his immediate needs as they arise. You will usually have to forget the lesson you have so carefully prepared and deal with something else more urgent—that will be your test as an extension-chain teacher: to be able to put your student's needs before what you would like to teach.

At first the men will learn only how to witness; then they will prepare new believers for baptism, organize the church, learn discipline, and serve the Lord's Supper. New believers should not preach. They can sing, pray, read the Bible, and give testimonies. Until there is someone ready to preach, the Lord's Supper should serve as the center of their worship. It will not corrupt new believers to serve the Lord's Supper, but it will swell their heads to preach. Let their preaching develop naturally out of their witnessing. First they win their friends by humbly presenting Christ, using their own Bibles. Soon they begin telling their friends Bible stories. Then they teach simple Bible studies, using the reteachable extension materials. Gradually that practice in communicating the Word evolves into preaching, and the stilted preaching manner provoked by premature pulpit assignments is avoided.

Remember, the local men raise up their own church, not you. Not any outside pastor! Break that rule and you break the extension chain. You will have a preaching point instead of a church: a sure dead-end link. Impress that continually on your student-workers.

d) Organize the church with only the essential requirements. The new congregation must be an obedient church, practicing *all* the things Christ commands His church (Matt. 28:18-20). Determine what those things are.

Three levels of authority for the churches provide a basis for determining whether you should require or prohibit any given practice:

(1) Divine commandments. Examples: faith, repentance, baptism, love,

170

sanctification, the Lord's Supper, prayer, giving, evangelism, biblical instruction of believers. Those are required. They cannot be prohibited.

(2) Apostolic practices. Examples: serving the Lord's Supper daily in homes, baptizing converts immediately upon profession of faith, sharing all goods in common, and so forth. Those are not required. Neither are they to be prohibited, for they are biblically sanctioned.

(3) Evangelical traditions. Examples: Sunday school, choirs, wearing a tie in the pulpit, catechism for baptismal candidates, ordination requirements, public invitations to "go forward," and so forth. Those are not to be required (Matt. 15:1-9). They may be prohibited if they impede obedience. Their only God-given authority is the voluntary agreement of a certain congregation (Matt. 18:18-20).

Direct all your teaching toward helping your student obey the simple commands of Christ for His churches. Never start a daughter church with detailed bylaws inherited from a mother church in a different area or you will produce a dead-end link. An extension chain will cross social and language barriers with little problem if you limit the new church requirements to the mere commandments of Christ.

4. TEACH AS CHRIST DID

a) Teach primarily by your own personal example. Like Christ, the teacher in an extension chain never asks his students to do anything they have not seen their teacher do first. You will have to walk to homes to witness if you expect your student to do it. The force of your example is the impetus for a live chain. Use only equipment and methods that your student can use. Do not raise up a church using films and then ask your student to do it without films. Do not preach from analytic outlines that require years of training and then ask him to preach simple messages because of his limited preparation. If you want him to preach simple messages, you had better do it too. Follow the example of Paul, who told his converts to imitate him.

b) Motivate your student by using an obedience-oriented curriculum. The student in an extension chain does not do his assignments for his teacher; he does them for Christ. All his studies aim at fulfilling Christ's commands. All the essential elements of the traditional curriculum are taught, but in their *functional* order. Doctrine, history, Bible, and so forth are introduced where they relate to the immediate needs of a growing, multiplying congregation. Long courses of several months must yield to weekly units that fulfill your student's changing needs. Two-week "core" units (one month in remote areas) can unite elements of different subjects in such a way that the average lay pastor can relate them to each other. The extension chain textbooklet *Atanasio*[1] unites church history, doctrine, polemics, and a homiletical exercise in one brief comic-book format and is small enough to be carried in the pocket and read little by little during the week for reteaching the following Sunday.

You need not motivate your extension-chain student with grades and diplomas. He does not "graduate" until his chain has produced a growing church in every town and neighborhood of his field of responsibility.

Do not make the *first* goal of your students doctrinal perfection. That invites pharisaism. We want doers of the Word and not hearers only. We need pastors, not pulpiteers. Keep the curriculum aimed primarily at obedience or you will produce dead-end links. An obedience-oriented curriculum is easy to prepare; the Bible is written that way: every doctrine is presented in a context that demands its corresponding practical duty.

c) Let each student progress at his own speed. The entire chain cannot study one standard course at the same time. The chain is too complex and teaching conditions too varied. One rigid system will not meet different students' needs.

d) Make sure that each week's study produces the most urgently needed practical work. If it is necessary, write your own materials that require immediate application. First list your educational objectives. Be sure that your list grows out of a careful study of the needs of your students, based primarily on the commands of Christ for His church. Then prepare weekly teaching units that will, in the shortest time possible, meet all the essential elements of the traditional seminary curriculum. But not in the same way! Do not try to deal with only *one* subject in each unit. Such teaching can never adapt to the vibrant, exciting, and novel involvements of a living chain.

You must build each unit of study around one specific activity done in fulfillment of one of the commandments of Christ for His church. That practical work is the "core." The core of a beginning unit would simply be *witnessing*. But it would teach things listed under several different educational objectives. Under "Bible" it partially fulfills the objective *knowledge of the gospels* as a study of the life of Christ to present Him to others. Under "Theology" it contributes to *knowledge of soteriology* as a study of the plan of salvation. Under "Personal Evangelism" it teaches some *knowledge of church-growth principles* as a study of to whom one should witness first (selection of good soils). Under "Pastoral Theology" it imparts some *knowledge of the duties of a church member* as a study of necessary follow-up activities involved in witnessing, in obedience to Christ. Such a curriculum requires much less textbook reading and classroom time. It permits frequent review of the same doctrines in varied contexts and applications. In my chain, it solved the problem of student motivation, both for studying and for practical work. To write such units, you must list your educational objectives on one axis of a large graph. (My graph nearly covers one wall. After almost every trip to the villages, I add some new objective to cover some urgent need.) On the other axis, list the weekly units you will teach. Then indicate under every unit all the possible objectives it can help meet. (See the abbreviated graph, figure 10.1.) You can teach such weekly units by assigning sections of regular extension textbooks, but you will need to supplement them, bringing in the other necessary elements to enable the men to do their assigned activity.

CORE ACTIVITIES (UNITS):

This example of a Curriculum Graph is too abbreviated for actual use.

Educational Objectives:	HAVE DAILY DEVOTIONS	WITNESS	CALL TO REPENTANCE	ASSURE NEW BELIEVERS	PREPARE FOR BAPTISM	ORGANIZE NEW CHURCH	PRESIDE AT SESSIONS	ELECT OFFICERS	MOBILIZE DEACONS	DEVELOP STEWARDSHIP	BEGIN MISSION PROJECT	BUILD CHAPEL	ORGANIZE GRAIN CO-OP	TRAIN INTERP. BIBLE	TEACH INDUCT. STUDY	COMBAT LEGALISM	MAINTAIN DISCIPLINE	COUNSEL DISCOURAGED	COUNSEL BACKSLIDDEN	DISCIPLINE OFFENDERS	DEFEND VS. ROM. CATHOLICISM
DEVELOPMENT OF SPIRITUAL LIFE																					
prayer	x				x																
separation from sin			x		x											x		x		x	x
stewardship						x		x		x	x	x	x								
KNOWLEDGE OF THE WORD																					
Bible survey, gen.														x							
hermeneutics														x	x						
O.T. intro.														x							
Pentateuch																					
history																	x				
poetry	x																				
prophets										x											
N.T. intro.														x							
gospels		x	x							x	x										x
Acts, epistles					x	x	x	x	x	x						x		x	x	x	x
KNOWLEDGE OF THEOLOGY																					
God, Trinity	x																				
soteriology		x	x	x													x			x	x
Christology		x								x											x
ecclesiology					x	x	x	x	x	x							x			x	x
etc.																					
KNOWLEDGE OF CHURCH HISTORY																					
ancient														x							x
medieval															x		x				x
Reformation			x											x	x						x
Latin American						x				x											x
DEVELOPMENT OF PASTORAL SKILLS																					
evangelism		x	x	x	x																
counseling				x														x	x	x	
Christian education														x							
discipline						x											x	x		x	x
administration						x	x	x	x	x		x					x				
etc.																					
FULLFILLMENT OF CHRISTIAN SOCIAL DUTIES																					
combat poverty										x		x									
etc.																					

*Notice that most of the units deal with several educational objectives. The one on having daily devotions makes use of instruction on prayer, Psalms, the worship of God (notice the x's after those educational objectives listed under "HAVE DAILY DEVOTIONS"). Normally the objectives would be far more detailed, to show exactly what each unit touches, and **primary** and **secondary** objectives would be shown.*

Figure 10.1

174

5. HELP EACH DAUGHTER CHURCH BECOME A MOTHER CHURCH AS WELL

a) Urge the newborn church to mobilize workers for continued reproduction. Keep extending the chain. Do not lose the happy momentum of spontaneous movement of church growth. Teach the new workers to obey the Great Commission. Ask the new church to send out workers to start their own daughter churches. Get an official vote for that.

b) Promote the extension students to student-teachers. Not every extension student has the capacity for being a student-teacher; but try each of them. The slower man may surprise you. It helps little to be bright if one cannot take heavy responsibility. Once he realizes that he stands at the head of a new section of the chain, a mediocre student will often start new churches with a zeal and facility that surpass his teacher's. But keep out of his way when he takes his first solo flight. Do not control his movements; let the work get out of your hands. Let him reteach the studies he has learned from you to his own new students (2 Tim. 2:2). Let him repeat everything he has seen you do, in the same way. He does not need to complete the entire pastoral course before he opens his own subcenter; he needs only to keep a unit ahead of his students. He teaches them what is still exciting in his own experience.

When a worker matures spiritually, his congregation may recognize him as pastor. He should have the laying on of hands, which gives him more confidence as an extension teacher. Do not hesitate to make such a layman an extension teacher. He has already helped raise up his own church in the chain (the one truly qualifying test to see if he can teach others to do the same).

c) Do not let building programs stop the chain (do not let anything stop it). In urban areas where new chapels cost too much to build, groups must meet in homes or rented halls as fast as a chain requires. When groups grow too big, they should divide. But you must teach them how to do it in an orderly manner, and the leadership for the newly divided congregation must be prepared ahead of time. Plan ahead!

d) Evaluate constantly the progress of each student and teacher in the chain.

(1) Keep a checklist on the studies and practical work of each student and teacher. Bring it up to date in each class. Each student-teacher also keeps a checklist for his own students and always gives a report of their progress to his own teacher.

(2) Analyze any dead-end links. Go over the entire list of steps to see where you failed. If the link is incurably broken, bypass it. Do not waste time with nonreproductive churches.

(3) Visit all the works regularly as a silent observer. Then send out reteachable materials that apply the Word to their current needs.

e) To continue the chain indefinitely, seek out student-teachers who will simply repeat those same steps. Student-teachers who will simply repeat the steps may lack pastoral experience and education, but they will be leaning on the principal. You must back them and encourage them. You might help pay their travel expenses. But above all, you must give them full responsibility in their own area. That Paul-Timothy relationship continues all down the chain. Give them the example to follow, then step back and let them do it. Each teacher must give full responsibility to his own Timothy. Do not let the teachers keep doing all the preaching in their subcenters. That is what they are training their students for! Do not let the whole church attend the extension class. Let the local student reteach what he has learned in the class to the rest of the people. If the extension teacher always preaches and directs in his students' place, he weakens their ministry and ends the chain. Once he gives the direction or preaching as an extension assignment, they do it from then on.

Here is how this program produced twenty-five new churches in northern Honduras between 1970 and 1973:

1970 ORIGINAL MOTHER CHURCHES	1971 *DAUGHTER CHURCHES	1972 **GRANDDAUGHTER CHURCHES	1973 ***GREAT-GRAND-DAUGHTER CHURCHES
Total churches in program	4	8	17	29
Total members of participating churches	205	295	450	760

By the end of 1979, the program had produced:

Great-great-granddaughter churches	8
Great-great-great granddaughter churches	4
Total churches in program	64
Total baptized members (approx.)	2020

Discussion Questions

1. What does the author mean by an *extension chain?* What basic steps are necessary in starting such a chain?
2. Define the three levels of authority for determining whether a practice is required or optional.
3. Discuss the merits of a *curriculum graph* in which core activities (units) are coordinated with educational objectives. In what ways could the use of such a graph be beneficial in each week's study?

1. Instituto Biblico de Extension, Apdo. 164, La Ceiba, Honduras.

11

LEADERSHIP: Key to the Growth of the Church

Lois McKinney

God is at work around the world. Churches are growing. They are experiencing spiritual renewal. They are reaching out. On the island of Java, people movements have swept one hundred thousand animistic Muslims to Christianity.[1] In the last forty years, sub-Saharan Africa has become substantially Christian.[2] In Brazil, the church is growing almost twice as fast as the population.[3] In some places, church growth may be painstakingly slow; in others it may be breathtakingly fast. In widely scattered places, through diverse means, and among hundreds of different peoples, Christ is building up His church.

The growth of the church is a reason for rejoicing; it is also a cause for deep concern. Concern? When the number of believers is multiplying and new churches are springing up every day? Yes, concern. As churches grow, the need for church leaders multiplies. In many areas of the world, existing

LOIS MCKINNEY (Ph.D., Michigan State University) is executive director of CAMEO (Committee to Assist Missionary Education Overseas). Dr. McKinney has served two terms in Portugal and one term in Brazil with the Conservative Baptist Foreign Mission Society. Loaned to CAMEO during her last term, she directed the Internships in Curriculum Development Program, which offers graduate level training in theological education by extension.

educational programs are not even beginning to meet the demand for trained leaders. In Brazil, the need is acute. My own estimate is that if that country continues to prepare church leaders at the present rate and through existing means, it will take forty years to prepare the leaders Brazilian churches need today.[4] That is not an isolated case. In country after country, many more church leaders are needed.

WHY IS LEADERSHIP DEVELOPMENT LAGGING BEHIND THE GROWTH OF THE CHURCH?

At the risk of oversimplifying complex issues, I would like to suggest a possible explanation for the lag in the development of church leaders overseas. First I shall present an ecclesiological example; then an educational example; and then the possible explanation.

AN ECCLESIOLOGICAL EXAMPLE: OVERRELIANCE ON A PROFESSIONAL CLERGY

Much of the work of overseas churches revolves around ordained clergy who are seminary trained and are paid for their ministry. In some cases, those leaders are doing their best to teach those who will teach others (2 Tim. 2:2). But in other cases they perceive themselves to be *the* ministers of the church rather than God's gifts to the church to equip the *laos*, the people of God, for the work of the ministry (Eph. 4:11-12). It is true that alternatives that would involve more of the Body in ministry are sometimes considered. There are lengthy debates about the possibilities for a plurality of elders, tent-making ministers, and women in ministry. But, for the most part, even in places where churches cannot afford to pay their pastors, the full-time, professional ministry remains the norm. Church leaders are being added one at a time from the ranks of seminary graduates instead of being multiplied as church members exercise the gifts God has given them within the Body of Christ. And the whole Body suffers.

AN EDUCATIONAL EXAMPLE: OVERRELIANCE ON RESIDENCE SEMINARIES

The residence seminaries in which most overseas pastors are trained are usually geared to reaching young, academically superior potential leaders who can dislocate themselves from their communities for three to five years of study. In some situations, those programs have been extremely effective. In others, they have been beset by problems: there is often a high attrition rate, and in many areas of the world the cost of maintaining those institutions has become prohibitively expensive. After observing theological education in the Philippines, Ted Ward, professor of education at Michigan State University, remarked, only half facetiously, that the only kind of professional preparation he knows about that is more expensive than overseas theological education is astronaut training.

My own observation coincides with Ward's. I know of one seminary in a developing country that invested approximately $80,000 a year in faculty and staff salaries (including those of expatriate missionaries), approximately $2,500 per year for each student in residence (the student body averaged ten per year), and around $20,000 a year on buildings and equipment. Those figures sound modest enough. It took $125,000 a year to keep the institution afloat. But the stated purpose of the school was to prepare denominational pastors for a rural area of the country. During the twenty-five years it was in operation, only six of the seminary's graduates entered pastorates in the region. The cost of preparing six rural leaders was an astronomical $3,125,000.

Beyond financial considerations, there is another more serious shortcoming inherent in traditional theological education. The academic level and the residence requirement often exclude those who most badly need a theological education, the mature leaders of congregations. Those recognized leaders are usually married men with limited formal schooling and little or no preparation for their church-related ministry. They have jobs to hold down and a wife and children to support. Their families and their churches depend on them. They cannot and should not be uprooted from their communities. For them, a residence seminary is not the answer. And since alternate modes of preparation are seldom provided, the church continues to suffer from a lack of developed leadership.

A CULTURAL EXPLANATION: EXPORTED NORMS

Happily, many church planters and theological educators overseas are recognizing the impediments to church leadership development that are created by an overreliance on a professional clergy and residence seminaries. Simultaneously, they are becoming aware that the crux of the problem is a cultural myopia that looks upon modes of theological education practiced in the United States, England, or Germany as being equally appropriate in Brazil, Kenya, or Indonesia. Somehow, in spite of verbal commitments to "indigenous principles," "nationalization," or "contextualization," Western systems for developing church leaders all too often are still the norm.

WHAT CAN BE DONE TO FREE OVERSEAS THEOLOGICAL EDUCATION FROM EXPORTED NORMS?

What can be done? How can overseas theological education be freed from inappropriate Western norms? Our answer to that question begins with the overseas churches themselves. They must assume the responsibility for developing their own leaders.

OVERSEAS CHURCHES MUST DISCOVER CULTURALLY AUTHENTIC FORMS OF WORSHIP, INSTRUCTION, FELLOWSHIP, AND OUTREACH

Because leadership development occurs in and through churches, one of the first tasks facing the overseas church that wants to develop its leaders is to discover culturally authentic forms of expression. What that means will vary from culture to culture. It may mean substituting guitars for organs or storefronts for steepled buildings. It is likely to involve more basic concerns, such as discovering redemptive analogies to employ in communicating the gospel,[5] or developing functional substitutes for non-Christian practices that have heavy loadings of cultural meaning.[6] So much has been said about those concerns recently that there is no need to belabor them here. They are mentioned to remind us that the church itself must reflect the cultural authenticity it wants to see in its leaders.

OVERSEAS CHURCHES MUST DECIDE HOW MANY AND WHAT KINDS OF LEADERS THEY NEED

As culturally authentic forms of church worship, instruction, fellowship, and outreach are discovered, a pattern for church leadership will begin to emerge. What kinds of leaders do the churches need? Will there be one elder or many elders? Will the church leaders receive salaries? How old should they be? Should they be men or women? Should they be married or single? Should they come from the same socioeconomic strata as the persons they are serving? What kinds of lives should they be living in their homes, their churches, and their communities? What are they expected to be able to do in their ministries? What kinds of skills, knowledge, and attitudes will they need to develop in order to minister? As those kinds of questions are asked, a portrait of leadership will come into focus. At first it may be blurred, and it may look suspiciously like an expatriate missionary or an iron-willed *caudillo* who rules their country. But gradually, as natural leaders are encouraged to exercise their spiritual gifts and as the Word of God is examined in cultural perspective, the overseas churches will discover the kinds of leaders they need.

The picture of leadership needs that emerges will reveal several categories of leaders, each with different functions.[7]

Level 1: local leaders. Local leaders are the persons who exercise teaching, preaching, administrative, and evangelistic functions within a local congregation.

Level 2: overseers of small congregations. Overseers of small congregations are those who hold a small congregation together or share in the direction of a larger congregation.

Level 3: overseers of a large congregation or of clusters of small congregations. Overseers of a large congregation or of clusters of small congregations often function as circuit-riding ministers to scattered groups of believers. In some cases, particularly in urban areas, they may lead one large congregation rather than several small ones.

Level 4: regional, national, and international administrators. Regional, national, and international administrators are the persons who tie associations of churches together.

Level 5: educator-scholars. Educator-scholars are specialists who exercise their influence upon the church through scholarly research and the development of theological disciplines.

Overseas churches will need to decide how many of those leaders are needed now and how many will be needed ten years from now. Realistic ratios might be one level 1 leader for every 5 church members, one level 2 leader for every 30 church members, and one level 3 leader for every 250 church members. Only a handful of leaders will be needed at levels 4 and 5. Projections of leadership needs will grow out of plans for church growth. If an association of churches intends to double its membership over a ten-year period, leadership needs will also double. At level 1, doubling a church's membership from

1,500 to 3,000 members will mean doubling the number of adequately prepared leaders from 300 to 600.[8]

OVERSEAS CHURCHES MUST DEVELOP THEIR OWN CURRICULA

When an overseas church is able to describe the leaders it needs, it is ready to begin developing a curriculum. That curriculum is not just a list of materials to be studied: it is a description of the competencies church leaders must have in order to minister effectively.

George Patterson has used a competency-based approach to curriculum development in Honduras. All of his students are planting churches. He meets with them regularly to discover the needs they are facing in their ministries. The needs that are identified determine the next lesson to be assigned. If the church planter/student is working with a group of believers who are ready to be baptized, the lesson for the week centers on the biblical teaching about baptism, how to prepare believers for baptism, and how to baptize. Lessons are practiced and the Word of God is obeyed. Education is for competency in ministry.[9]

Similar to Patterson's approach is growth contracting, an individualized mode of curriculum development that has been attempted quite successfully in the master's degree program at the Baptist Theological Faculty in Sao Paulo, Brazil, in an in-service development program at Gordon College, in at least one theological school in Southeast Asia, and in other contexts and places as well. The plan is simple: the students (who are often university professors or other professional persons) engage in a process of self-evaluation to discover areas in which they need to grow. They develop proposals that describe (1) their current status, (2) what they would like their status to be at the end of the year (or at the end of the program, or at the end of the course), and (3) how they expect to get from their current status to their desired status. The proposals include descriptions of persons, materials, workshops, and field experiences that are available as resources. Guidance committees are enlisted, and the growth contracts are submitted to an educational institution (or other directing body) for approval. Regular reports of progress toward growth goals are made to the committees and institutions.[10]

The impact of those individualized kinds of approaches to curriculum development on the preparation of church leaders overseas could be far-reaching. The course of study should be built around reflection upon the Word of God in the context of day-by-day experiences in ministry. In Brazil, leaders will discover what it means to minister in a society influenced by Roman Catholicism, spiritism, *machismo,* and rapid urbanization. In Hong Kong, they will be concerned with ministry in the midst of Eastern religions, Communism, Westernization, and new opportunities on the Chinese mainland. The aim of that kind of reflection and action is the development of competency-based, contextualized curricula. And the desired result is the emergence of leaders who are authentically Latin or African or Asian and who can minister uniquely and effectively in their own cultures.

OVERSEAS CHURCHES MUST DEVELOP APPROPRIATE STRUCTURES FOR PREPARING THEIR LEADERS

Efforts to train church leaders inevitably take on shape and form. The most common structure to emerge is a residence seminary. God has blessed that mode of instruction. Thousands of church leaders around the world are the products of residence programs. No one can deny that a high quality of training can be and is being provided at them. But as I pointed out earlier, those programs have serious limitations: they are usually dependent on foreign funding, and they train only limited numbers of young people who can be dislocated from their own communities. Alternatives are needed that will make available training that does not involve cultural dislocation and for which overseas churches can afford to pay.

Such alternatives are available. Night schools function well in urban centers. Intensive, short-term institutes are feasible in many rural areas. In remote regions of the world, radio broadcasts, cassette tapes, or printed materials can be coupled with regular meetings among peers and occasional visits from professors. In almost all situations, church activities such as Bible-study groups can become vehicles for the development of church leadership. Internship programs are sometimes possible. One-to-one tutorial and discipling relationships can be effective. Theological education by extension (TEE) will function wherever students and teachers can meet together.

A word of caution is in order here. Educational programs must begin with students, not with structures. Too often the location of the school is chosen first. Then a faculty is enlisted, buildings are constructed, and a curriculum is planned. Of course a library is set up. Then, after everything else has been done, someone remembers to ask, "Where are the students?" or, "Who will be able to attend our school?" Obviously, a culturally sensitive approach to leadership development must reverse the process. The target group of students must be identified *first*. A careful study must be made to discover where they are, what their needs are, when and where they can study, and how much study time they have available. With those kinds of data in hand, churches will be in a much better position to create appropriate structures for preparing their leaders for ministry.

Any discussion of alternate structures for theological education sooner or later raises questions about educational standards. With accrediting associations springing up around the world, those questions are being asked more frequently and more urgently. The assumption seems to be that academic quality can be maintained only through residence programs. One need only to look at the Open University in England, in-service programs for medical doctors, or Doctor of Ministry programs in seminaries to realize that many nonresidence programs encourage quality in academic performance.

The crux of the problem is at another level: how to determine the academic equivalence of programs pursued through different modes. There are at least two workable solutions to that problem. One is to substitute the traditional credit system, based on hours spent in a classroom, with a credit system that takes into account the hours the student spends in all kinds of learning activities. That is already being done by schools that grant credit for internships and independent studies. Another solution is to substitute the credit system with a competency-based examination system. Students would demonstrate that they have developed competencies they need for their ministries. When and how they developed the competencies, and the academic credits they received in the process, would become largely irrelevant. Competency-based evaluation has been practiced for years in European universities and in certain professions in the United States. For some reason, however, ecclesiastical bodies have turned their evaluative function over to seminaries. Ordination is often based on completion of the Master of Divinity degree rather than on competency in ministry.

OVERSEAS CHURCHES MUST DEVELOP CULTURALLY ATTUNED METHODS OF TEACHING

Even though overseas churches may have a clear picture of the kinds of leaders they need, and even though they may have adequate curricula and structures to prepare those leaders for ministry, they may still fall short of their educational goals if culturally attuned teaching methods are not employed. Teaching methods must be attuned to cultural values, to the ways people learn, and to their life experiences.

Teaching must be attuned to cultural values. Expatriate missionaries tend to interpret what they see overseas in the light of experiences in their homelands. I still remember my reactions to churches when I was a new missionary in Portugal. I shuddered at the authoritarian teaching methods, at the meetings that dragged on for hours, at the persons with gray hair who were attending youth meetings, and at the poems and plays that were presented so often that I wondered if people came to church to be entertained.

In retrospect, I realize that those practices expressed traditional cultural values. Portuguese believers felt comfortable when they were respecting authority, relating to an extended family, appreciating drama, and enjoying time instead of using it. It was my own ethnocentricity that made it difficult for me to see the implications of those values for teaching. What I discovered in Portugal applies in other cultures as well. Teaching must be attuned to cultural values.

Teaching must be attuned to the ways people learn. Even though we intuitively sense that persons in different cultures learn in different ways, and even though studies have been undertaken in several research traditions, we still know very little about crosscultural differences in learning.

That does not mean that progress has not been made. Cross-cultural studies within the framework of Piaget's developmental theory point toward both invariability of progressive stages of development and differences in the time required to develop from one stage to another.[11] That means that some adult learners with limited schooling may not have reached Piaget's formal or abstract stage of operations. Those who work with semiliterate church leaders will need to be careful to reach those learners where they are, teaching them through concrete, activity-oriented experiences in ministry, and—at the same time—helping them to sharpen their thinking skills.

Another interesting group of studies focuses on field-dependent and field-independent cognitive styles.[12] Field-dependent learners rely upon surrounding elements in performing a thinking task; field-independent learners can more readily isolate elements from their surrounding field. There is some limited evidence that a tendency toward field-dependence and field-independence may vary from culture to culture. If that is true, it would help us to understand why an African who has learned to perceive reality holistically has such a difficult time trying to understand what a book written by an analytically-minded North American is trying to say.

Other interesting insights into cross-cultural learning patterns have come through ethnopedagogical research in which teaching rather than learning is studied. For example, in my doctoral research I explored the relative effectiveness of expository and discovery methods of programmed instruction with semiliterate adults in Brazil.[13] One of the interesting findings was that the discovery method was more effective with adults who had taught themselves to read, whereas the expository method was more effective with those who had learned to read in school. That finding suggests that discovery teaching is more closely attuned to the way some people learn than are the expository methods that have been imported along with formal schooling.

Programmed instruction (PI) was an effective vehicle for my research in Brazil because it was carefully developed, frame by frame, in across-the-table tests with informants. Through their active responses to programmed items, I was able to observe thinking processes and attune instruction to the ways the students had learned to learn.

The extensive use of PI in theological education by extension has made the evangelical world aware of the potential applications of the method in the development of leaders for the church. Unfortunately, that awareness has not been accompanied by an understanding of PI as a teaching instrument that can be precisely attuned to cultures and as a potentially dangerous tool if it is tied to behavioristic presuppositions. That ignorance has resulted in some disastrous efforts to translate programs from one language to another or mold and shape the behavior of learners. But in spite of its limitations and its misapplications, PI has often provided an efficient means of transmitting the informational component of instruction and certain kinds of skills to students who must study on their own. In the process, it has freed the weekly meetings of theological education by extension from boring lectures and made them into valuable times of discussion.

Teaching must be attuned to life situations. Cultures transmit their heritage from one generation to another through song, dance, drama, rituals, and other means. Those forms of cultural expression provide useful data in determining which teaching methods are likely to be effective. In northeastern Brazil, *jograis* (a traditional kind of poetry recited by a verse choir) should not be overlooked. In the United States, there are many teaching possibilities in epoch dramas—*Roots*, for example. A good starting point in attuning teaching methods to life situations is to observe how culture is transmitted in nonschool settings.

Another good step to take in attuning teaching methods to life situations is to encourage students to gather their own cultural data and make their own cultural applications. I have used that procedure often in my own teaching. On one occasion in northeastern Brazil, for example, I asked students to make as long a list as they could of all the objects they would find in an interior home and courtyard. Then I asked them to describe how any ten of those objects could be used in teaching. The students were enthusiastic. One young man commented, "I feel sorry for teachers in cities where they don't have all these interesting things to work with!"

Some Western methods can be attuned to other cultures. Case studies, role-playing, and instructional simulations are all based on life situations. They can be effective teaching methods in many different contexts. Certain other group methods are also applicable cross-culturally if they are freed from Western norms for interaction—expecting a group leader always to keep a low profile, for example. Careful observation of informal groups (e.g., gathering of neighbors in front of a house) and more structured groups (e.g., a meeting of community leaders to resolve a problem) can provide clues to the kinds of interaction that are likely to be most effective in a given culture.

SUMMARY AND CONCLUSION

In many parts of the world, leadership development is lagging behind the growth of the church. Possible explanations include overreliance on Western norms, such as a professional clergy and residence seminaries.

What can be done to free overseas theological education from innappropriate Western norms? The answer begins with the overseas churches. They must discover culturally authentic forms of worship, instruction, fellowship, and outreach. They must decide what kinds of leaders they need. They must develop the curricula, structures, and methods that are needed to prepare their leaders for ministry.

The church is at the center of God's plan for the world. It is within the church that leaders are prepared for ministry. It is through the church that Christ's commands are obeyed. It is to the church that Christ has given His promises. He will be with us while we are making disciples—with us always, even to the end of the age!

Discussion Questions

1. Comment on the author's two examples and explanation of why leadership development lags far behind the growth of the church overseas. Are they valid in your area of responsibility? Do they rule out any paid clergy? Residence seminaries?

2. Is the author's premise that responsibiltiy for developing leadership must be assumed by local churches tenable? If so, discuss each of the five suggestions for freeing theological education from exported norms and their practical implications at the local-church level.

1. Donald A. McGavran, "Church Growth Around the World," *Asia Theological News* (October 1978), pp. 14-15.

2. Ibid.

3. William R. Read and Frank A. Ineson, *Brazil 1980: The Protestant Handbook* (Monrovia, Calif.: Missions Advanced Research and Communications Center (MARC), 1973), p. 125.

4. There are at least 10,000,000 evangelicals in Brazil. My estimate is that 1 in 50—that is, 200,000—of that number are or should be leaders of their congregations, and at least 50 percent of those leaders—100,000 of them—are untrained. Seminaries and Bible institutes are graduating no more than 2,500 students annually. At that rate it would take forty years to train the leaders the Brazilian church needs today.

5. The most celebrated example of that process has been Don Richardson's "peace child" analogy.

6. At the Asian Leadership Conference on Evangelism, held in Singapore November 1-10, 1978, a pastor from Taipei told us about the functional substitutes his church

has developed for the Chinese New Year activities. All the key elements of the festival—worship, family gatherings, parties, and wishing friends success in the new year—were included in a Christian celebration.

7. The categories of leadership described here have been adapted from leadership levels identified by McGavran.

8. For a more complete description of means of estimating leadership needs, see Lois McKinney, "Plan for Church's Leadership Needs," *Evangelical Missions Quarterly* 11, no. 3 (July 1975): 183-87.

9. George Patterson's approach to developing leaders is described in his booklet *Obedience-oriented Education,* available through the Church Growth Book Club, 1705 Sierra Bonita Avenue, Pasadena, California 91104.

10. Further information is available in the *Professional Development Through Growth Contracts Handbook* (Wenham, Mass.: Gordon College, 1979).

11. Pierre R. Dasen, ed., *Piagetian Psychology: Cross-cultural Contributions* (New York: Gardner, 1977) provides a compilation and summary of those studies.

12. This research is reviewed in H. A. Witkin et al., "Field-Dependent and Field-Independent Cognitive Styles and Their Educational implications," *Review of Educational Research* 47, no. 1 (Winter 1977): 1-64.

13. Lois McKinney, "Cultural Attunement of Programmed Instruction: Individualized-Group and Expository-Discovery Dimensions" (Ph.D. diss., Michigan State University, 1973).